Grade 8

Addison-Wesley Mathematics

Practice Workbook

 Addison-Wesley Publishing Company

Menlo Park, California ■ Reading, Massachusetts ■ New York
Don Mills, Ontario ■ Wokingham, England ■ Amsterdam ■ Bonn
Sydney ■ Singapore ■ Tokyo ■ Madrid ■ San Juan

ISBN 0-201-27803-0 ♻ Text printed on recycled paper.

11 12 13 14 15 - HC - 95

Table of Contents

Understanding Place Value

Write each number in standard form.

1. 104 thousand

_____

2. 22 million

_____

3. 4.7 thousand

_____

4. 68.1 billion

_____

5. 249 thousand

_____

6. 49.93 thousand

_____

7. 7.03 million

_____

8. 2.658 billion

_____

9. 0.16 billion

_____

10. 127.6 thousand

_____

Write each number in terms of its largest place value period name.

11. 24,000,000

_____

12. 156,000

_____

13. 12,500

_____

14. 1,110,000

_____

15. 7,000,000,000

_____

16. 2,760,000,000

_____

17. 7,737,000

_____

18. 27,730,000,000

_____

Name _____

Numerical Expressions

Use the basic properties to evaluate each numerical expression.
Name the property you used.

1. $608 \times 1 = \boxed{}$

_____

2. $362 + \boxed{} = 362$

_____

3. $26 \times 51 = 1,326$

$51 \times 26 = \boxed{}$

_____

4. $17 + (54 + 12) = 83$

$(17 + 54) + 12 = \boxed{}$

_____

5. $5 \times (6 + 3) = 45$

$(5 \times 6) + (5 \times 3) = \boxed{}$

_____

6. $(22 \times 4) + (22 \times 6) = 220$

$22 \times (4 + 6) = \boxed{}$

_____

7. $92 \times \boxed{} = 92$

_____

8. $77 \times 32 = 32 \times \boxed{}$

_____

9. $28 + 0 = \boxed{}$

_____

10. $219 \times 0 = \boxed{}$

_____

Name each of the properties described.

11. The way in which addends or factors are grouped does not change the result.

_____

12. Changing the order of addends or factors does not change the sum or the product.

_____

13. The sum of any given number and 0 is the given number.

_____

14. The product of any given number and 1 is the given number.

_____

Reviewing Mental Math

Use counting on or back or compatible numbers to evaluate each expression using mental math.

1. $44 + 2$

2. $74 + 20$

3. $159 + 21 + 17$

_____   _____   _____

4. $248 + 10$

5. $6.4 + 2.6 + 1.8$

6. $21 + 29 + 33$

_____   _____   _____

Break apart numbers or use compensation to evaluate each expression using mental math.

7. 29×2

8. 21×5

9. 52×6

_____   _____   _____

10. 102×5

11. 39×3

12. 73×2

_____   _____   _____

Evaluate using mental math. Name the technique you used.

13. $7.5 + 1.5 + 2.8$

14. 33×2

15. $79 + 30 - 6$

_____   _____   _____

_____   _____   _____

16. 71×3

17. $134 - 20 + 5$

18. 49×4

_____   _____   _____

_____   _____   _____

19. The Johnson family spends an average of $100 on groceries each week. How much do they spend on groceries each year?

_____

PS-8

Name _____

Reviewing Estimation Techniques

Estimate. Use rounding to substitute compatible numbers.

1.   109
      + 661

2.   1,724
       −   390

3. $91,282
       − 24,630

4. $761
        182
      + 244

5.   2,503
        1,877
      + 5,050

6.   8,756
       − 1,593

Estimate. Use front-end estimation.

7. $9,511
       − 3,454

8.   742
        106
      + 335

9.   16,802
        14,124
      + 17,910

Estimate.

10.   927
        − 615

11.   659
        + 280

12.   568
        − 177

13.   347
        + 715

Estimate.

14. The area covered by the Mediterranean Sea is 2,965,800 km^2. The area covered by the Bering Sea is 2,291,900 km^2. About how much larger is the Mediterranean Sea?

15. The area of the Gulf of Mexico is about 1,582,800 km^2. Estimate the total area of the Gulf of Mexico and the Bering Sea.

16. The area of the Caribbean Sea is about 2,718,200 km^2. About how much larger is the Mediterranean Sea?

17. Use the data about the Mediterranean Sea, the Gulf of Mexico, the Bering Sea, and the Caribbean Sea to write your own problem.

Name _____

Introduction to Problem Solving

Use the 6-point checklist to help you solve each problem.

To Solve a Problem
1. Understand the Situation.
2. Analyze the Data.
3. Plan What to Do.
4. Estimate the Answer.
5. Solve the Problem.
6. Examine the Answer.

1. The flying distance from Chicago to San Francisco is 2,975 km. The distance from San Francisco to Honolulu is 3,840 km. What is the total flying distance from Chicago to Honolulu?

2. The flying distance from London to Berlin is 933 km. The flying distance from Berlin to Warsaw is 515 km. What is the total distance from London to Warsaw?

3. The flying distance from New Delhi to Hong Kong is 3,742 km. The flying distance from New Delhi to Cairo is 4,413 km. How much longer is the flying distance from New Delhi to Cairo than from New Delhi to Hong Kong?

4. The flying distance from Beijing to Caracas is 14,320 km. The flying distance from Melbourne to Caracas is 15,550 km. How much farther is Caracas from Melbourne than from Beijing?

5. The flying distance from New York to Bangkok is 13,870 km. The flying distance from Bangkok to San Francisco is 12,690 km. What is the total flying distance from New York to San Francisco via Bangkok?

6. The flying distance from Stockholm to Rio de Janeiro is 10,692 km. The flying distance from Stockholm to Washington, D.C., is 10,865 km. How much farther is it to Stockholm from Washington, D.C., than from Rio de Janeiro?

Using Critical Thinking

Decide whether each of the following answers is
correct or incorrect. If it is incorrect, tell what is wrong
with the method used.

1.
$$\begin{array}{r} 40 \\ 7\overline{)280} \\ -28 \\ \hline 0 \\ 0 \\ \hline 0 \end{array}$$

2.
$$\begin{array}{r} 23 \\ \times\ 5 \\ \hline 1{,}015 \end{array}$$

3.
$$\begin{array}{r} 14 \\ \times\ 6 \\ \hline 24 \\ 6 \\ \hline 30 \end{array}$$

_____   _____   _____

_____   _____   _____

_____   _____   _____

4.
$$\begin{array}{r} 14 \\ 14 \\ 14 \\ 14 \\ 14 \\ +\ 14 \\ \hline 30 \end{array}$$

5.
$$\begin{array}{r} 15\ R2 \\ 6\overline{)38} \\ 6 \\ \hline 32 \\ 30 \\ \hline 2 \end{array}$$

_____   _____

_____   _____

_____   _____

6. $12 \times 84 = 1{,}008$ so

$21 \times 48 = 1{,}008$

7. $36 \times 42 = 1{,}512$ so

$63 \times 24 = 1{,}512$

_____   _____

_____   _____

_____   _____

Order of Operations

Find the value of each expression. Use the order of operations.

1. $2 \times (8 - 1) \times 2$ _____   **2.** $16 \div 8 \times 7 - 4$ _____

3. $6 + 27 \div 9 + 8$ _____   **4.** $32 \div 8 \div 2$ _____

5. $15 \div 5 + 6 \times 2$ _____   **6.** $4 \times 3 - 2 \times 5$ _____

7. $8 \times 4 - 3 \times 5$ _____   **8.** $5 \times (3 + 2)$ _____

9. $56 \div 7 \times 3$ _____   **10.** $25 \div 5 - 1 \times 3$ _____

11. $2 \times 5 - (16 \div 4 + 2)$ _____   **12.** $30 \div 2 \div 5 + 1$ _____

13. $3 \times (15 - 8)$ _____   **14.** $(5 + 8 \times 2) \div 7$ _____

15. $54 \div 9 \times 6$ _____   **16.** $7 \times 2 - 6 \div 3$ _____

17. $17 + 4 \times 2 + 2$ _____   **18.** $10 \times 4 \div 8$ _____

19. $20 + 8 \div 4 - 4$ _____   **20.** $21 \div (49 \div 7) + 1$ _____

21. $15 \div 3 + 7 \times 2$ _____   **22.** $6 + (3 \times 4) + 2$ _____

23. $(6 + 3) \times (4 + 2)$ _____   **24.** $(17 - 9) \times 4 - 1$ _____

25. $5 + 6 \div 3 \times 4$ _____   **26.** $15 + 3 - 2 \times 5$ _____

27. $42 \div 6 + 3 \times 1$ _____   **28.** $5 \times (8 - 4) + 7$ _____

29. $10 - (40 \div 8)$ _____   **30.** $(12 - 4) \div (2 \times 2)$ _____

31. $5 \times 4 - 3 \times 6$ _____   **32.** $5 \times 9 - 6$ _____

33. $48 \div 8 \div 3$ _____   **34.** $15 - (36 \div 9) + 5$ _____

35. $(17 - 3) \div 7$ _____   **36.** $21 - (5 + 6)$ _____

Name _____

Relating the Operations

Write an addition equation that is related to each of
the following.

1. $10 - 1 = \boxed{}$ _____

2. $25 - 13 = \boxed{}$ _____

3. $50 - 16 = \boxed{}$ _____

Write a multiplication equation that is related to each
of the following.

4. $42 \div 7 = \boxed{}$ _____

5. $100 \div \boxed{} = 50$ _____

6. $120 \div 20 = \boxed{}$ _____

7. Write two subtraction equations you can solve if you know $81 + 34 = 115$.

_____   _____

8. Write two division equations you can solve if you know $89 \times 6 = 534$.

_____   _____

Write an addition, subtraction, multiplication,
or division equation for each of the following.

9. 13 groups of 7 _____

10. 6 rows with 12 in a row _____

11. What number added to 43 is 156? _____

12. How many 15s are in 390? _____

13. What number multiplied by 12 is 252? _____

14. A dozen dozen eggs _____

Name _____

Developing a Plan

Decide if you need an exact answer or an estimate.
Then determine the best calculation method and
solve the problem.

1. There are 17,056 rivers, streams, and lakes in the United States.
According to the Environmental Protection Agency, 584 of
them were polluted by industrial facilities by the middle of 1989.
How many waterways were not polluted?

Solution: _____   Method: _____

2. West Virginia has the most waterways (1,745), Wisconsin is
second with 1,124, and Minnesota is third with 1,140. What is
the total number of waterways in all three states?

Solution: _____   Method: _____

3. 63% of Massachusetts's 29 waterways are polluted. Of
Tennessee's 269 waterways, 6.3% are polluted. Which state has
more polluted waterways? How many more?

Solution: _____   Method: _____

4. Roger wants to rent 4 videotapes for the weekend. Each rental
costs $3.15 including tax. If he has $12.11, does he have enough
money?

Solution: _____   Method: _____

5. Michelle's father is dividing his collection of 465 comic books
evenly among Michelle and her two sisters and two brothers.
How many comic books will each person receive?

Solution: _____   Method: _____

Algebraic Expressions

Evaluate each expression for $a = 6$, $b = 5$.

1. $6 + a$

2. $7b$

3. $a - 4$

4. $\dfrac{30}{b}$

5. $40 - 5a$

6. $\dfrac{a}{3}$

7. $a + b$

8. ab

9. $a - b$

10. $\dfrac{a + 4}{b}$

11. $2a + b$

12. $\dfrac{b}{a - 1}$

Complete each table by evaluating the expressions.

	c	$6c - 2$
13.	1	
14.	3	
15.	5	
16.	10	

	d	$\dfrac{d + 2}{4}$
17.	10	
18.	18	
19.	26	
20.	30	

	f	$60 - 4f$
21.	2	
22.	5	
23.	7	
24.	9	

	s	t	$2s + t$
25.	7	4	
26.	5	9	
27.	3	6	
28.	4	4	

	m	n	$3m + 4n$
29.	8	10	
30.	15	24	
31.	7	9	
32.	10	8	

Divided Bar Graphs

Use the divided bar graph to answer Questions 1–5.

1. Which day do the most boys and girls

attend computer class? _____

3. On what days do the fewest number of
boys and girls attend class?

_____

4. On which day does the class have an
equal number of boys, girls, and

adults? _____

5. Make a divided bar graph to represent
the data below. First decide what the
highest and lowest numbers you need

to show are. _____

Favorite subjects of a 9th-grade class

	Boys	Girls
Math	7	3
History	2	4
English	4	4
Reading	0	2
Science	5	5

2. What is the number of: boys   girls
adults   who attend class on Friday?

_____ _____ _____

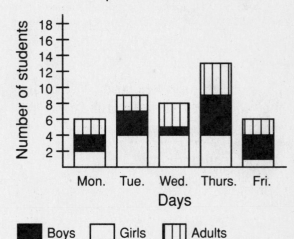

Computer Class Attendance

Name _____

Circle Graphs

Use the circle graph to answer questions 1–5.

Uses of Electrical Energy in One Home

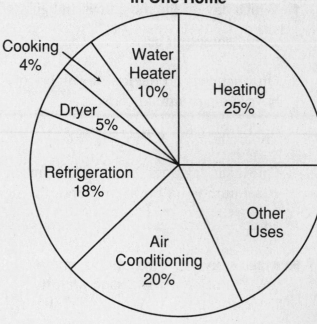

1. What single item used the most energy?

   _____

2. What percent of the energy was for "Other uses"?

   _____

Suppose the cost of electrical energy for one month was $124. Find the cost for each use.

3. Air-conditioning _____

4. Cooking _____

5. Refrigeration _____

Use the circle graph to answer each question. Suppose the cost of electrical energy is $180 a month. Find the cost for each electrical use.

Electrical Energy Usage

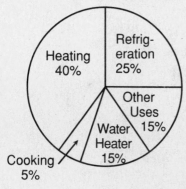

6. Heating _____

7. Refrigeration _____

8. Cooking _____

9. Water heater _____

10. Other uses _____

Name _____

Stem and Leaf Tables

1. The batting averages of the 13 players on the Kennedy Junior High baseball team were: .335, .333, .292, .277, .328, .297, .328, .280, .267, .280, .265, .280, and .321. Complete the stem and leaf table to organize the data.

Stem	Leaf

2. How many leaves does the 32 stem have?

   _____

3. Which stems have no leaves?

   _____

4. What is the highest batting average? _____

5. Which average appears more frequently, .280 or .328? _____

6. The Metro Junior High players' averages were: .261, .289, .304, .282, .336, .312, .285, .322, .302, .284, .336, .277, and .333. In the box, make a stem and leaf table of the batting averages.

7. How many players on both teams batted in the .280s?

   _____

8. How many on both teams batted higher than .300?

   _____

9. How many batted less than .300?

Name _____

Frequency Tables and Histograms

The 30 leading hitters in the Junior High School
Baseball League got the following numbers of hits: 76,
108, 60, 74, 116, 88, 68, 74, 108, 76, 78, 93, 116,
108, 68, 88, 108, 60, 74, 68, 88, 78, 76, 108, 116, 84,
106, 96, 93, and 96.

1. Make a stem and leaf table in the box to organize
the data.

2. Use your stem and leaf table to complete the
frequency table below.

Frequency Table	
Grouping Intervals	Frequency
60–69	
70–79	
80–89	
90–99	
100–109	
110–119	

3. Make a histogram in the space at the
right to show the data in the frequency
table.

4. What is the range of number of hits?

_____

5. In which interval do the greatest
number of players appear?

_____

Name _____

Using Critical Thinking

Use the data to draw both bar graphs.
Then answer each question.

KC Computer Chip Stock

Week	1	2	3	4	5
Price	$24.00	$23.25	$23.00	$22.75	$22.00

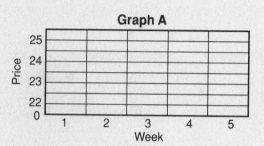

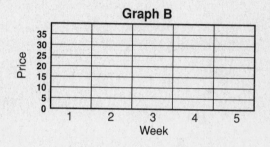

1. What is the difference in the price of stock from the first week to the fifth week?

_____

2. Looking at the size of the bars on Graph A, it appears that the price of the stock at the first week is how much more than the price at the fifth week?

_____

3. Is Graph A misleading? Explain.

_____

_____

Use the data below to draw two different bar graphs. Label one graph so that the size of the bars appear to show misleading data. Label the other graph so the size of the bars is not misleading.

Ralley Athletic Shoe Stock

Week	1	2	3	4	5
Price	$15.00	$14.50	$14.00	$13.50	$12.00

Mean, Median, and Mode

Find the mean, median, and mode of each list of numbers.

1. 16
  23
  14
  16
  21
  16
  20

mean: _____

median: _____

mode: _____

2. 118
  120
  116
  120
  131

mean: _____

median: _____

mode: _____

3. 746
  289
  311
  624
  335
  119

mean: _____

median: _____

mode: _____

4. 252
  622
  715
  398
  252
  164
  320

mean: _____

median: _____

mode: _____

5. 44
  19
  44
  38
  17
  44
  11

mean: _____

median: _____

mode: _____

6. $5.46
  3.12
  2.00
  5.15
  2.00
  1.69
  2.00

mean: _____

median: _____

mode: _____

7. 1,020
  890
  445
  615
  1,020

mean: _____

median: _____

mode: _____

8. $12.00
  14.14
  14.14
  6.75
  9.31
  12.00

mean: _____

median: _____

mode: _____

9. 197
  245
  317
  712
  114
  401

mean: _____

median: _____

mode: _____

Box and Whisker Graphs

Draw a box and whisker plot for each set of data.

1. 2.3, 4.2, 4.6, 5.9, 6.4, 6.9, 7.3, 7.4, 8.0, 8.3, 8.8, 10.3

2. 40, 44, 19, 100, 79, 56, 31, 43

3. 335, 332, 331, 314, 326, 325, 326, 314, 307, 304, 306, 332

4. 71, 79, 86, 77, 71, 80, 83, 79, 79, 80, 75, 77

Significant Digits and the Mean

Find the mean of each set of data and list of numbers.
Round to the correct number of significant digits.

1. {16, 23, 14, 16, 24, 16, 20}

_____

2. {118, 120, 116, 120, 134}

_____

3. 197.0
245.6
317.7
712.0
114.4
401.5

_____

4. 5.46
3.12
2.00
5.15
2.00
1.69
2.00

_____

5. 746
289
319
624
335
119

_____

6. 12.00
14.14
14.14
6.75
9.31
12.00

_____

7. 250
622
715
398
252
164
320

_____

8. 1,020
805
3,445
615
1,020

_____

9. {44.0, 19.0, 44.6, 38.0, 17.1, 44.5, 11.0}

_____

10. {4,444; 555; 66}

_____

Round to 1-digit accuracy.

11. 0.793 _____

12. 0.6088 _____

13. 3.82 _____

14. 28.74 _____

15. 0.053 _____

16. 0.0231 _____

17. 0.1875 _____

18. 0.00786 _____

19. 14.98 _____

Name _____

Understand the Question

Solve. Use any problem solving strategy. If it helps, ask each question in a different way.

1. Suppose that your fingernails grow 0.4 mm each day. How much will they grow in 30 days?

2. Steve's mass is 2.1 times as much as that of his dog Friday. Friday's mass is 20 kg. What is Steve's mass?

3. Suppose that your hair grows 0.3 cm each day. How much will it grow in 90 days?

4. Lana jogs 4.5 km every other day. How far will she jog in the month of June?

5. A customer bought 3 shirts for $9.95 each and a shirt for $12.50. What was the total amount spent?

6. A carpenter cut 8 pieces of board, each 0.42 m long, from a board that was 3.6 m long. How much of the board was left over?

7. A phonograph record turns 45 times per minute. How many times would that record turn in playing a song that is 2.6 minutes long?

8. The air distance from Atlanta to San Francisco is 3,442 km. A pilot flew 5 round-trip flights in one month. How far did the pilot fly that month?

9. Josie rode her unicycle 1.25 hours. Her rate of travel was about 6 km per hour. How far did she ride the unicycle?

10. It took 5 strips of wallpaper, each 71 cm wide, and one strip 42 cm wide to cover a wall of a room. What was the width of the wall covered by the wallpaper?

Evaluating Expressions

Evaluate these expressions.

1. $7a + 4$ for $a = 6$

2. $\dfrac{m}{6} + 8$ for $m = 24$

3. $9n - 7$ for $n = 7$

_____   _____   _____

4. $3k + 6$ for $k = 8$

5. $\dfrac{x}{8} - 3$ for $x = 48$

6. $\dfrac{s}{10} + 16$ for $s = 50$

_____   _____   _____

7. $\dfrac{b}{7} + 7$ for $b = 49$

8. $15y - 40$ for $y = 5$

9. $\dfrac{v}{12} - 4$ for $v = 120$

_____   _____   _____

10. $20p + 5$ for $p = 5$

11. $3b + 10$ for $b = 33$

12. $\dfrac{e}{5} - 9$ for $e = 70$

_____   _____   _____

When the expression $\dfrac{9}{5}C + 32$ is evaluated for C,
it describes the number of degrees F. Find °F for
each exercise.

13. $C = 20°$ **14.** $C = -30°$ **15.** $C = 0°$ **16.** $C = 100°$

_____   _____   _____   _____

17. $C = -90°$ **18.** $C = 45°$ **19.** $C = -45°$ **20.** $C = 25°$

_____   _____   _____   _____

Area

Use square units and triangles to estimate the area of
each region.

1.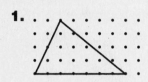

_____ square units

2.

_____ square units

3.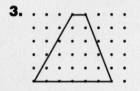

_____ square units

4.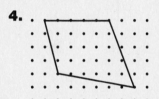

_____ square units

5.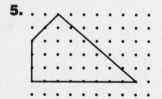

_____ square units

6.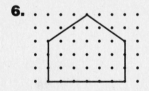

_____ square units

7.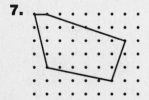

_____ square units

8.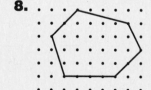

_____ square units

Name _____

Area of Polygons

Find the area of each polygon.

1.

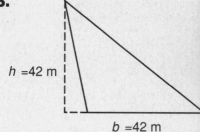

58 cm, h = 44 cm

Area = _____

2.

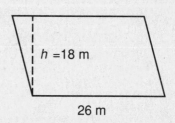

h = 18 m, 26 m

Area = _____

3.

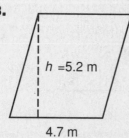

h = 5.2 m, 4.7 m

Area = _____

4.

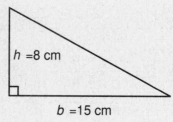

h = 8 cm, b = 15 cm

Area = _____

5.

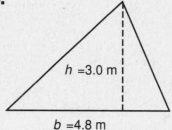

h = 3.0 m, b = 4.8 m

Area = _____

6.

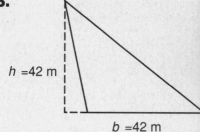

h = 42 m, b = 42 m

Area = _____

7.

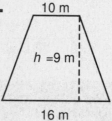

10 m, h = 9 m, 16 m

Area = _____

8.

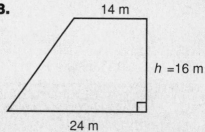

14 m, h = 16 m, 24 m

Area = _____

9.

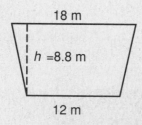

18 m, h = 8.8 m, 12 m

Area = _____

Name _____

Using the Strategies

Solve each problem. Use Guess and Check or Draw a Picture.

1. Mr. Ruiz divided his square garden into 4 equal parts. He then divided each of these parts into 4 more equal parts. How many squares did he have when he finished?

_____

2. The area of the foundation of a new house is 760 ft². The perimeter is 116 ft. What are the dimensions of the foundation?

_____

3. Cara weighs 1 pound less than Greg. The product of their weights is 2,970 lb. What are their weights?

_____

4. Kim has 3 more coins than Nikki. The product of their numbers of coins is 648. How many coins does each girl have?

_____

5. A picture frame is 8 inches longer than it is wide. If the area is 468 square inches, what are the dimensions of the frame?

_____

6. The rectangle below is divided in thirds. Keep one third intact, divide one in half, and divide the last one in fifths. How many sections are there?

_____

PS-8

Name _____

Using Critical Thinking

Examine the 5 regular polyhedra. Then complete the table.

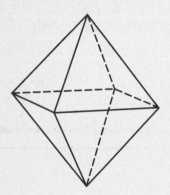
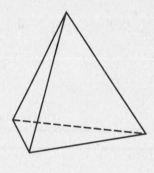
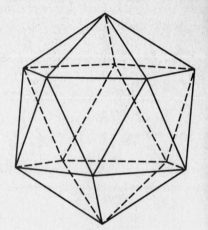

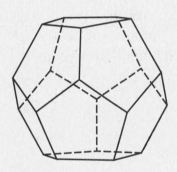
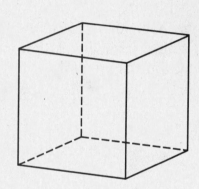

Polyhedron	Number Faces	Type of Polygon Used
tetrahedron	4	triangle
1. hexahedron	_____	_____
2. octahedron	_____	_____
3. dodecahedron	_____	_____
4. icosahedron	_____	_____

Name _____

Volume of Prisms and Cylinders

Find the volume of each prism. Use the formula $V = Bh$.

1.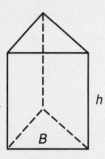

$B = 10 \text{ cm}^2$
$h = 12 \text{ cm}$

$V = $ _____

2.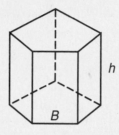

$B = 36 \text{ m}^2$
$h = 8 \text{ m}$

$V = $ _____

3.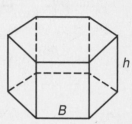

$B = 50 \text{ m}^2$
$h = 16 \text{ m}$

$V = $ _____

Find the volume of each rectangular prism. Use the formula $V = lwh$

4. $l = 6 \text{ m}$
  $w = 5 \text{ m}$
  $h = 4 \text{ m}$

  $V = $ _____

5. $l = 7 \text{ cm}$
  $w = 6 \text{ cm}$
  $h = 5 \text{ cm}$

  $V = $ _____

6. $l = 12 \text{ m}$
  $w = 10 \text{ m}$
  $h = 8 \text{ m}$

  $V = $ _____

7. $l = 4.2 \text{ m}$
  $w = 2.6 \text{ m}$
  $h = 6.0 \text{ m}$

  $V = $ _____

8. $l = 6.7 \text{ cm}$
  $w = 2.8 \text{ cm}$
  $h = 4.0 \text{ cm}$

  $V = $ _____

9. $l = 5.3 \text{ cm}$
  $w = 2.7 \text{ cm}$
  $h = 4.0 \text{ cm}$

  $V = $ _____

Find the volume of each cylinder. Use the formula $V = \pi r^2 h$.

10.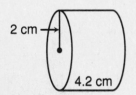

2 cm

4.2 cm

$V = $ _____

11.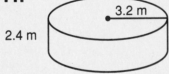

3.2 m

2.4 m

$V = $ _____

12.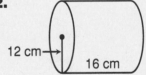

12 cm

16 cm

$V = $ _____

13. $r = 4 \text{ cm}$
  $h = 7 \text{ cm}$

  $V = $ _____

14. $r = 10 \text{ m}$
  $h = 8 \text{ m}$

  $V = $ _____

15. $r = 1.2 \text{ cm}$
  $h = 6 \text{ cm}$

  $V = $ _____

Name _____

Volume of Pyramids and Cones

1. Find the volume of this cylinder. (Leave the volume in terms of π.)

   _____

2. Use the formula $\frac{1}{3}\pi r^2 h$ to find the volume of the cone inscribed in the cylinder. (Leave the volume in terms of π.)

   _____

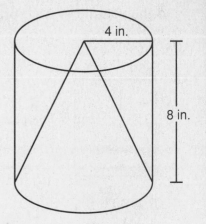

4 in.

8 in.

3. What is the ratio of the volume of the cone to the volume of the cylinder in the figure above?

   _____

4. If the cylinder above is cut in half so the height is 4 inches, what will be the volume of an inscribed cone?

   _____

5. Find the volume of this prism and its inscribed pyramid.

   _____   _____

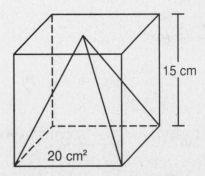

15 cm

20 cm²

6. What would be the volume of this prism if it had a base of 10 cm²?

   _____

7. What would be the volume of its inscribed pyramid?

   _____

8. What other dimensions might a pyramid equal in volume to $\frac{1}{2}$ the volume of the pyramid in Exercise 7 have?

   _____

Solving Equations

Solve these equations using mental math.

1. $15 + x = 25$

_____

2. $35 + m = 65$

_____

3. $b - 56 = 89$

_____

4. $b - 67 = 103$

_____

5. $5t = 620$

_____

6. $3k = 189$

_____

7. $\frac{2}{3}g = 12$

_____

8. $\frac{1}{9}n = 100$

_____

9. $x + 23 = 143$

_____

10. $y + 89 = 156$

_____

11. $k - 25 = 109$

_____

12. $t - 20 = 190$

_____

13. $6p = 126$

_____

14. $8r = 648$

_____

15. $\frac{3}{4}w = 27$

_____

16. $36 = 2t$

_____

17. $25 = \frac{5}{6}m$

_____

18. $67 = y - 12$

_____

Write an equation for each scale below. Solve the
resulting equation using mental math.

_____   _____   _____

_____   _____   _____

Name _____

Using the Strategies

Solve. Use any strategy.

1. Alaska's population is 522,000. That is 3,778,000 less than the population of Maryland. What is the population of Maryland?

2. The population of the United States is 238.7 million. California with 26.3 million, New York with 17.7 million, and Texas make up 25.26% of the U.S. total. What is the population of Texas?

3. Ohio's population is 0.625 million less than the mean population of Florida (11.3 million), Illinois (11.5 million), and Pennsylvania (11.8 million). What is the population of Ohio?

4. To the nearest million, find the mean of the populations of Iowa (2.8 million), New Hampshire (0.998 million), Vermont (0.535 million), Hawaii (1.0 million), Massachusetts (5.8 million) and Nevada (0.94 million).

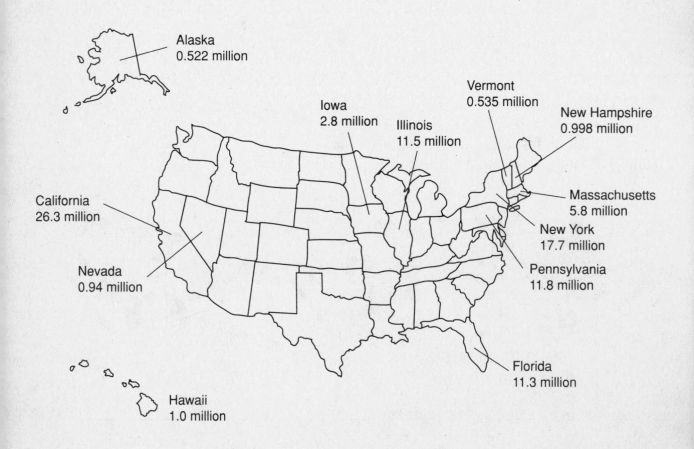

Alaska
0.522 million

Vermont
0.535 million

New Hampshire
0.998 million

Iowa
2.8 million

Illinois
11.5 million

Massachusetts
5.8 million

California
26.3 million

New York
17.7 million

Nevada
0.94 million

Pennsylvania
11.8 million

Florida
11.3 million

Hawaii
1.0 million

Inverse Operations

Show the inverse operation needed to simplify each
expression so the variable is the result.

1. $y - 14$

_____

2. $\dfrac{x}{8}$

_____

3. $k + 49$

_____

4. $43 \cdot 2d$

_____

5. $\dfrac{z}{12}$

_____

6. $h - 34$

_____

7. $n + 476$

_____

8. $w - 3 \cdot 23$

_____

9. $g \div 14$

_____

10. $a - 95 \cdot 3$

_____

11. $m - \dfrac{5}{8}$

_____

12. $86.3y$

_____

13. $g + 58.2$

_____

14. $\dfrac{c}{8}$

_____

15. $76x$

_____

16. $x - 121$

_____

17. $\dfrac{x}{12}$

_____

18. $a + 3.7$

_____

19. $b \div 14$

_____

20. $15c$

_____

21. $3d$

_____

One-Step Equations

Solve and check these equations.

1. $19x = 38$

2. $4.4 + y = 10.4$

3. $\dfrac{n}{3} = 13$

_____

_____

_____

_____

4. $y - 46 = 32$

5. $8.4a = 25.2$

6. $\dfrac{w}{6} = 72$

_____

_____

_____

_____

7. $\dfrac{b}{13} = 26$

8. $c - 4\dfrac{1}{3} = 5\dfrac{2}{3}$

9. $7x = 49.7$

_____

_____

_____

_____

Name _____

Problem Solving: Data from a Table

Solve. Use any problem solving strategy. Use data
from the loan table.

1. Mr. Allaire bought a new car for
$18,000. He received a credit of
$12,000 for the car he traded in. How
much did he finance and how much
will he have paid after 24 months?

_____

2. Ms. Linn wants to buy a car that costs
$26,000. She has a down payment of
$14,000. What will be her monthly
payment?

_____

Automobile Financing at 11.50% for 24 months	
Loan Amount	Monthly Payment
$6,000	$281.09
7,000	327.94
8,000	374.79
9,000	421.63
10,000	474.06
11,000	533.01
12,000	599.28
13,000	673.81
14,000	757.59
15,000	851.79
16,000	957.71

3. Mrs. Sullivan paid $12,792.24 over the
life of her loan. What were her monthly
payments? How much did she borrow?

_____

4. If Mrs. Sullivan had borrowed $10,000
instead of $11,000, how much less
would she have paid back at the end of
24 months?

_____

5. How much interest would you have to
pay for a car loan of $7,000?

_____

6. How much more interest would you
have to pay on a loan of $9,000 than
on an $8,000 loan?

_____

Name _____

Using Critical Thinking

Complete the table and look for a pattern for each
situation. You may want to draw a picture.

1. The number of sections formed by points on a line
if no point is placed at an end of the line

Points	Sections
1	
2	
3	
4	

Pattern _____

_____

2. The number of sections formed by points on a
circle

Points	Sections
1	
2	
3	
4	

Pattern _____

3. The number of sections formed by segments
through a rectangle if the segments all intersect at
one point

Points	Sections
1	
2	
3	
4	

Pattern _____

_____

4. The number of sections formed by segments
through a rectangle if each segment intersects
exactly one other segment

Points	Sections
1	
2	
3	
4	

Pattern _____

_____

Name _____

Two-Step Expressions

Write the steps that show how you build and undo
these expressions.

	Build	Undo
1. $3h + 1.7$		
2. $7v - 10$		
3. $2u + 9$		
4. $4d + \dfrac{1}{5}$		
5. $\dfrac{a}{9} - 17$		
6. $4s - 13$		
7. $\dfrac{m}{2} + 11$		
8. $1.7x - 3.2$		
9. $6n + 15.1$		
10. $\dfrac{t}{3} - 1$		
11. $\dfrac{b}{2} - 4$		
12. $27p + 81$		

Two-Step Equations

Solve the equations.

1. $7a + 4 = 46$

2. $\dfrac{m}{6} + 8 = 12$

3. $9n - 7 = 56$

_____

_____

_____

_____

4. $3k + 6 = 30$

5. $\dfrac{x}{8} - 3 = 3$

6. $\dfrac{s}{10} + 16 = 21$

_____

_____

_____

_____

7. $\dfrac{b}{7} + 7 = 14$

8. $15y - 40 = 35$

9. $\dfrac{v}{12} - 4 = 6$

_____

_____

_____

_____

10. $20p + 5 = 105$

11. $3b + 10 = 109$

12. $\dfrac{e}{5} - 9 = 5$

_____

_____

_____

_____

Inequality Relations

Using the symbols $<$, $\leq$, $>$, or $\geq$, find all the ways to
replace the question mark to make a true statement.

1. 2 ? 3 _____

2. 7 ? 7 _____

3. 15 ? 2 _____

4. 1.2 ? 2.1 _____

5. 11 ? 0 _____

6. 6 ? 6 _____

Find all solutions to each inequality selected from the
set of numbers: 0, 1, 2, 3, 4.

7. $y < 3$ _____

8. $c + 3 \geq 0$ _____

9. $y \leq 3$ _____

10. $x > 10$ _____

11. $t \geq 4$ _____

12. $n \leq 6$ _____

13. $x - 2 > 1$ _____

14. $3n + 1 > 2$ _____

15. $m + 1 > 2$ _____

16. $4x + 1 < 5$ _____

17. $m + 1 \geq 2$ _____

18. $\frac{x}{2} \leq 1$ _____

19. $8 - y < 5$ _____

20. $10 - y > 8$ _____

Algebra

Name _____

Functions

1. If it costs \$2 per hour to park a car at the airport, the cost to park can be expressed as the function $c = 2t$. Complete the table to find the cost of parking the car over a span of 1-5 hours.

time (t)	1	2	3	4	5
$c = 2t$					

2. Jonathan is 24 years younger than his mother. His mother's age can be expressed as $M = 24 + J$. Complete the table to find his mother's age at different ages in Jonathan's life.

Jonathan's age (J)	1	5	10	12	16
$M = 24 + J$					

Complete each table of values for the given function.

3.

b	0	4	5	8	9
$V = 4b + 7$					

4.

x	3	6	9	12	15
$F = \dfrac{x}{3} + 5$					

5.

n	1	3	5	7	9
$R = 2(n + 1) - 3$					

6.

p	2	5	8	11	14
$E = 8(p - 1) - 3$					

Name _____

Function Tables

Complete each table of input-output pairs for these function rules.

1. function rule: $n + 4$

n	$f(n)$
1	
2	
3	
4	
5	

2. function rule: $2n + 5$

n	$f(n)$
1	
2	
3	
4	
5	

3. function rule: $92 - 4n$

n	$f(n)$
1	
2	
3	
4	
5	

4. function rule: $4(n + 1)$

n	$f(n)$
1	
2	
3	
4	
5	

5. function rule: $\dfrac{n + 2}{3}$

n	$f(n)$
1	
2	
3	
4	
5	

6. function rule: $\dfrac{7n - 5}{4}$

n	$f(n)$
1	
2	
3	
4	
5	

Name _____

Graphing Functions

For each of the following functions, complete the table of input-output values. Then graph the functions.

1. $y = x - 1$

x	1	2	3	4	5
y					

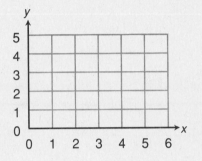

2. $y = 2x + 1$

x	0	$\frac{1}{2}$	1	$\frac{3}{2}$	2
y					

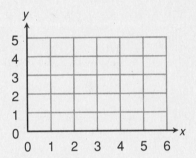

3. $y = \frac{3}{x}$

x	1	2	3	4	5
y					

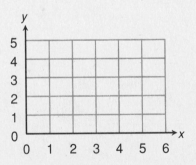

4. $y = x - \frac{1}{x}$

x	1	2	3	4	5
y					

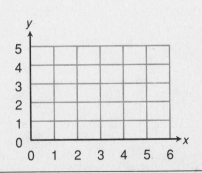

Skills Maintenance

Name _____

Exponential Notation

Write each expression as a standard numeral.

1. 12^0 _____

2. 9^3 _____

3. 2^7 _____

4. 5^2 _____

5. 10^4 _____

6. $(0.4)^3$ _____

7. 47^1 _____

8. $(0.1)^2$ _____

9. 10^5 _____

10. 30^3 _____

11. 88^0 _____

12. $(0.3)^4$ _____

13. $(0.2)^3$ _____

14. $4,812^0$ _____

15. 6^3 _____

16. $(0.5)^1$ _____

17. 20^2 _____

18. 8^4 _____

Write each expression in exponential notation.

19. $7 \cdot 7 \cdot 7 \cdot 7 \cdot 7 \cdot 7$ _____

20. $3 \cdot 3 \cdot 3 \cdot 3 \cdot 3 \cdot 3 \cdot 3 \cdot 3$ _____

21. $10 \cdot 10 \cdot 10$ _____

22. $(2.4) \cdot (2.4) \cdot (2.4) \cdot (2.4)$ _____

23. $5 \cdot 5 \cdot 5 \cdot 5 \cdot 5 \cdot 5 \cdot 5 \cdot 5 \cdot 5$ _____

24. $17 \cdot 17 \cdot 17 \cdot 17 \cdot 17$ _____

25. $24 \cdot 24 \cdot 24 \cdot 24$ _____

26. $(9.3) \cdot (9.3)$ _____

27. $2 \cdot 2 \cdot 2 \cdot 2 \cdot 2 \cdot 2 \cdot 2 \cdot 2 \cdot 2 \cdot 2$ _____

28. $10 \cdot 10 \cdot 10 \cdot 10 \cdot 10 \cdot 10$ _____

Write the missing exponent in each expression.

29. $4^4 \cdot 4^2 = 4$

30. $7^3 \cdot 7^1 = 7$

31. $15^1 \cdot 15^2 = 15$

32. $(0.2)^2 \cdot (0.2)^5 = (0.2)$

33. $8^0 \cdot 8^5 = 8$

34. $10^4 \cdot 10^4 = 10$

35. $6^6 \cdot 6^2 = 6$

36. $(0.3)^2 \cdot (0.3)^3 = (0.3)$

37. $5^2 \cdot 5^1 = 5$

38. $3^8 \div 3^3 = 3$

39. $9^4 \div 9^2 = 9$

40. $11^6 \div 11^4 = 11$

41. $(0.5)^7 \div (0.5)^3 = (0.5)$

42. $10^9 \div 10^5 = 10$

43. $2^8 \div 2^8 = 2$

44. $3^7 \div 3^6 = 3$

45. $5^3 \div 5^1 = 5$

46. $(0.1)^5 \div (0.1)^2 = (0.1)$

Name _____

Integers and Absolute Value

Write the opposite of each integer.

1. $^-42$ **2.** $^+17$ **3.** $^+4.83$ **4.** $^-6.01$ **5.** $^-46$

_____   _____   _____   _____   _____

6. $^+12.34$ **7.** $^-12.34$ **8.** $^+0.001$ **9.** $^-768$ **10.** $^+15.02$

_____   _____   _____   _____   _____

Use > or < to show which is greater.

11. 64 _____ 21   **12.** 24 _____ 16   **13.** 50 _____ $^-84$ **14.** 2 _____ $^-52$

15. 21 _____ 35   **16.** $^-23$ _____ $^-8$ **17.** $^-17$ _____ $^-84$ **18.** 24 _____ $^-24$

Find the absolute value of each number.

19. $|34|$ _____   **20.** $|^-75|$ _____   **21.** $|9.2|$ _____   **22.** $|^-12|$ _____

23. $|^-2,374|$ _____   **24.** $|^-12.9|$ _____   **25.** $|^-6.53|$ _____   **26.** $|^-34|$ _____

Complete each statement.

27. _____ $+ ^-42 = 0$ **28.** $5 + ^-5 =$ _____   **29.** $^-9 +$ _____ $= 0$

30. $17 +$ _____ $= 0$ **31.** _____ $+ 5.2 = 0$ **32.** $^-12.1 +$ _____ $= 0$

Identify the integer that is:

33. 5 less than $^-42$ _____   **34.** 3 greater than $^-15$ _____

35. 17 less than $^-17$ _____   **36.** 17 greater than $^-17$ _____

37. 23 less than $^+21$ _____   **38.** 11 greater than $^-22$ _____

Name _____

Addition of Integers

Find the sums.

1. $2 + {}^-4 =$ _____ **2.** $0 + {}^-8 =$ _____ **3.** $3 + {}^-3 =$ _____

4. ${}^-2 + {}^-3 =$ _____ **5.** ${}^-3 + 1 =$ _____ **6.** ${}^-7 + 2 =$ _____

7. ${}^-3 + 8 =$ _____ **8.** ${}^-7 + 3 =$ _____ **9.** ${}^-1 + 4 =$ _____

10. $1 + {}^-7 =$ _____ **11.** ${}^-8 + 2 =$ _____ **12.** $3 + {}^-2 =$ _____

13. $9 + {}^-4 =$ _____ **14.** ${}^-10 + 1 =$ _____ **15.** ${}^-1 + 1 =$ _____

16. ${}^-3 + {}^-5 =$ _____ **17.** ${}^-6 + 3 =$ _____ **18.** ${}^-7 + {}^-2 =$ _____

19. $1 + {}^-6 =$ _____ **20.** $3 + {}^-4 =$ _____ **21.** ${}^-1 + {}^-2 =$ _____

22. $4 + {}^-2 =$ _____ **23.** ${}^-8 + 1 =$ _____ **24.** ${}^-1 + 3 =$ _____

25. $8 + {}^-2 =$ _____ **26.** ${}^-2 + {}^-3 =$ _____ **27.** ${}^-1 + {}^-9 =$ _____

28. ${}^-8 + {}^-1 =$ _____ **29.** $3 + {}^-8 =$ _____ **30.** ${}^-3 + {}^-4 =$ _____

31. $5 + {}^-9 =$ _____ **32.** ${}^-2 + {}^-8 =$ _____ **33.** ${}^-3 + 6 =$ _____

Find the sums.

34. $6 + {}^-7 + {}^-3 =$ ___ **35.** ${}^-2 + {}^-4 + 5 =$ ___ **36.** ${}^-1 + 0 + 8 =$ ___

37. $3 + {}^-3 + 8 =$ ___ **38.** ${}^-9 + 5 + {}^-2 =$ ___ **39.** $7 + {}^-4 + {}^-2 =$ ___

40. ${}^-5 + {}^-3 + 8 =$ ___ **41.** ${}^-2 + {}^-3 + {}^-5 =$ ___ **42.** $5 + 4 + {}^-6 =$ ___

43. $4 + {}^-7 + 5 =$ ___ **44.** ${}^-2 + 0 + {}^-9 =$ ___ **45.** ${}^-8 + 1 + {}^-1 =$ ___

46. $7 + {}^-2 + {}^-5 =$ ___ **47.** ${}^-5 + 3 + {}^-7 =$ ___ **48.** $6 + 8 + {}^-4 =$ ___

Subtraction of Integers

Subtract.

1. $3 - {}^-6 =$ _____ **2.** ${}^-3 - {}^-2 =$ _____ **3.** ${}^-2 - 1 =$ _____

4. ${}^-5 - {}^-1 =$ _____ **5.** $1 - {}^-3 =$ _____ **6.** $2 - 5 =$ _____

7. $5 - {}^-1 =$ _____ **8.** ${}^-4 - {}^-2 =$ _____ **9.** ${}^-3 - 4 =$ _____

10. $0 - 3 =$ _____ **11.** ${}^-6 - 1 =$ _____ **12.** ${}^-1 - 4 =$ _____

13. ${}^-9 - {}^-6 =$ _____ **14.** $2 - {}^-7 =$ _____ **15.** ${}^-3 - {}^-5 =$ _____

16. $3 - {}^-4 =$ _____ **17.** ${}^-1 - {}^-3 =$ _____ **18.** $5 - {}^-6 =$ _____

19. $4 - {}^-5 =$ _____ **20.** ${}^-8 - 1 =$ _____ **21.** $0 - 6 =$ _____

22. ${}^-4 - {}^-1 =$ _____ **23.** ${}^-5 - 1 =$ _____ **24.** $3 - 7 =$ _____

25. $0 - {}^-4 =$ _____ **26.** ${}^-2 - {}^-3 =$ _____ **27.** ${}^-6 - {}^-3 =$ _____

28. ${}^-4 - 2 =$ _____ **29.** $4 - 6 =$ _____ **30.** ${}^-2 - 7 =$ _____

31. ${}^-6 - {}^-1 =$ _____ **32.** $8 - {}^-2 =$ _____ **33.** ${}^-4 - 4 =$ _____

Perform the operations inside the parentheses first.

34. $(5-2) + {}^-9 =$ _____ **35.** $({}^-3 - {}^-1) - {}^-5 =$ _____ **36.** $9 + ({}^-5 - {}^-6) =$ _____

37. ${}^-7 + (8-5) =$ _____ **38.** $(10 - {}^-3) - 12 =$ _____ **39.** $(8 + {}^-7) - {}^-4 =$ _____

40. $(3-5) - 6 =$ _____ **41.** $({}^-3 - {}^-4) - {}^-8 =$ _____ **42.** $({}^-11 + {}^-3) - {}^-2 =$ _____

43. $(8-10) - {}^-1 =$ _____ **44.** $(10-4) - 3 =$ _____ **45.** $(7-9) - 4 =$ _____

46. $({}^-5 + {}^-1) - 6 =$ _____ **47.** ${}^-2 + (3 - {}^-2) =$ _____ **47.** $(8 - {}^-1) - 4 =$ _____

Multiplication and Division of Integers

For each exercise, decide if the quotient will be a
positive or a negative number.
Write an equation and solve each problem.

1. Over a 5-day period, the stock market index decreased by 30 points. What was the
average change in the index per day?

_____

2. 4 days ago the stock market was 20 points higher than it is today. What is the average
change in the index per day?

_____

3. There were 48 fewer businesses in Allentown 3 years ago than there are today. What
is the average change in the number of businesses per year?

_____

4. 6 stores have opened in Allentown in the last 3 years. What is the average number of
stores that have opened per year?

_____

Use the exercises above as a model. What can you
conclude about the sign of each quotient?

5. When dividing two numbers with like signs, the quotient is _____.

6. When dividing two numbers with unlike signs, the quotient is _____.

Find the quotients.

7. $^-25 \div 5 =$ _____

8. $28 \div {}^-4 =$ _____

9. $40 \div {}^-8 =$ _____

10. $^-54 \div {}^-9 =$ _____

11. $^-15 \div 3 =$ _____

12. $32 \div 4 =$ _____

13. $72 \div {}^-8 =$ _____

14. $^-9 \div {}^-3 =$ _____

15. $56 \div {}^-7 =$ _____

16. $\dfrac{60}{^-6} =$ _____

17. $\dfrac{^-27}{3} =$ _____

18. $\dfrac{^-18}{^-6} =$ _____

19. $\dfrac{35}{7} =$ _____

20. $\dfrac{42}{^-6} =$ _____

21. $\dfrac{^-9}{^-9} =$ _____

Perform the operations inside the parentheses first.

22. $(^-5 + {}^-5) \div {}^-2 =$ _____

23. $^-3 + (21 \div {}^-3) =$ _____

24. $(^-56 \div 2) \div {}^-4 =$ _____

25. $63 \div (^-3 \times {}^-3) =$ _____

Using Critical Thinking

Determine which of the following statements are true (t) and which are false (f). Rewrite the false statements to make them true. a, b, and c are positive.

1. $^-a \cdot b = c$

_____

2. $^-a \cdot {}^-b = c$

_____

3. $a \cdot {}^-b = {}^-c$

_____

4. $a \cdot b = c$

_____

5. $^-a \cdot {}^-b = {}^-c$

_____

6. $a \cdot b = {}^-c$

_____

7. If a is negative and b is positive, then the product of a and b is positive.

_____

8. If the product of a and b is negative and a is negative, then b is positive.

_____

9. If a is positive and b is positive, then the product of a and b is negative.

_____

10. Complete the chart.

Integer a	Absolute Value of a	Integer b	Absolute Value of b	$a + b$	$a \cdot b$
3	3	$^-5$	5	$^-2$	$^-15$
$^-7$		$^-23$			
415		$^-2$			
$^-12$		$^-12$			
9		10			

Use with text page 138.

Solving Equations Using Mental Math

Use mental math to solve these equations.

1. $^-7n = 49$

_____

2. $^-6y = 12$

_____

3. $15a = 30$

_____

4. $\dfrac{n}{6} = 12$

_____

5. $^-19c = 0$

_____

6. $3x = ^-180$

_____

7. $x + 11 = ^-20$

_____

8. $y + ^-4 = 7$

_____

9. $21 - n = ^-13$

_____

10. $\dfrac{x}{^-6} = 2$

_____

11. $\dfrac{x}{6} = ^-2$

_____

12. $1 = \dfrac{y}{^-15}$

_____

13. $\dfrac{72}{y} = ^-6$

_____

14. $\dfrac{^-49}{a} = 7$

_____

15. $\dfrac{^-49}{a} = ^-7$

_____

16. $y + ^-46 = 0$

_____

17. $^-46 - y = 0$

_____

18. $46y = 0$

_____

19. $\dfrac{73}{a} = ^-1$

_____

20. $\dfrac{^-73}{a} = ^-1$

_____

21. $\dfrac{^-73}{a} = 1$

_____

Solving One-Step Equations

Solve these equations.

1. $k + {}^-5 = 7$

_____

_____

2. $g - {}^-2 = {}^-12$

_____

_____

3. $m + 2 = {}^-9$

_____

_____

4. $q + 4 = {}^-3$

_____

_____

5. $j - 5 = {}^-3$

_____

_____

6. $x + 8 = {}^-1$

_____

_____

7. $p - {}^-7 = 0$

_____

_____

8. $f + 6 = {}^-2$

_____

_____

9. $t - 7 = {}^-1$

_____

_____

10. $8s = {}^-56$

_____

_____

11. $\dfrac{v}{9} = {}^-4$

_____

_____

12. $^-3n = {}^-18$

_____

_____

13. $7h = {}^-35$

_____

_____

14. $\dfrac{r}{{}^-4} = 5$

_____

_____

15. $^-9f = 54$

_____

_____

16. $\dfrac{c}{{}^-2} = 15$

_____

_____

17. $^-8e = 88$

_____

_____

18. $\dfrac{w}{12} = {}^-5$

_____

_____

Name _____

Solving Two-Step Equations

Solve.

1. $^-4r - 3 = ^-27$

2. $8t + 9 = ^-15$

3. $\dfrac{m}{3} - 5 = 3$

4. $^-7q + ^-6 = ^-62$

5. $\dfrac{f}{-2} - 4 = ^-2$

6. $10f + ^-8 = 22$

7. $\dfrac{z}{3} - 8 = ^-4$

8. $^-1n + 15 = 11$

9. $\dfrac{t}{6} + 2 = ^-3$

Name _____

Using the Strategies

Solve. Write an equation.

1. A number is multiplied by 8, resulting in 40. What is the number?

_____

_____

2. Mr. Yen's weight increased by 14 pounds to 188.5 pounds. What was his original weight?

_____

_____

3. Over a 30-day period, the House of Pizza sold a total of 3,600 pizzas. What was the average number of pizzas sold per day?

_____

_____

4. Of the total number of pizzas sold during the 30 days, 2,000 were cheese pizzas, 500 were pepperoni pizza, and the rest were all other kinds. How many "other" pizzas were sold?

_____

_____

5. The result of dividing a number by 3.2 is 21.12. What is the number to the nearest hundredth?

_____

_____

6. The number of students in Ms. Acre's class increased by 2 on Monday and decreased by 3 on Friday. If there were 26 students in her class at end of the day on Friday, how many students did she have originally?

_____

_____

7. The quotient of a number divided by ⁻9 is 9. What is the number?

_____

_____

8. An integer is 3 greater than ⁻15. What is the number?

_____

_____

9. Identify the integer that is 27 less than ⁻27.

_____

_____

Name _____

Graphing with Integers

Write the coordinates of each point.

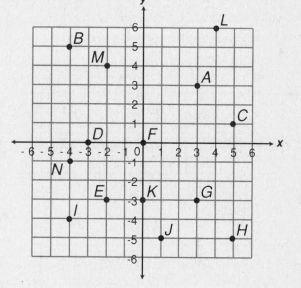

1. A _____   2. B _____

3. C _____   4. D _____

5. E _____   6. F _____

7. G _____   8. H _____

9. I _____   10. J _____

11. K _____   12. L _____

13. M _____   14. N _____

Plot these points on the coordinate plane.

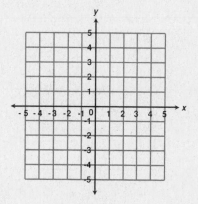

15. A _____   16. B _____

17. C _____   18. D _____

19. E _____   20. F _____

21. G _____   22. H _____

Draw line segments to connect these
pairs of points on the coordinate plane.

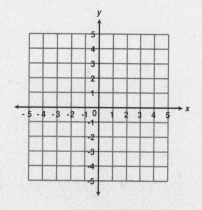

23. $(0, 3)$ to $(3, 0)$

24. $(^-1, 5)$ to $(^-5, 5)$

25. $(2, 4)$ to $(^-4, 2)$

26. $(^-3, ^-1)$ to $(^-3, ^-3)$

27. $(^-3, ^-3)$ to $(3, 0)$

28. $(0, 0)$ to $(5, ^-5)$

Name _____

Ordered Pairs That Solve Equations

Complete each of the following tables of input-output values.

1. $y = x + 3$

x	$^-4$	$^-2$	0	2	4
y					

2. $y = {}^-2x$

x	$^-4$	$^-2$	0	2	4
y					

3. $y = 2x - 1$

x	$^-1$	1	3	5	6
y					

4. $y = 5 - x$

x	$^-1$	1	3	4	5
y					

5. $y = 3x$

x	$^-3$	$^-2$	$^-1$	0	1
y					

6. $y = 3x - 4$

x	$^-3$	$^-2$	$^-1$	0	1
y					

7. $y = x$

x	$^-4$	$^-2$	0	2	4
y					

8. $y = {}^-x$

x	$^-4$	$^-2$	0	2	4
y					

9. $y = {}^-7 - x$

x	$^-4$	$^-2$	0	2	4
y					

10. $y = {}^-3x + 5$

x	$^-4$	$^-2$	0	2	4
y					

Name _____

Graphing Linear Functions

Complete each table of input-output values.
Then graph each pair of linear functions.

1. $y = x$

x	⁻3	⁻2	⁻1	1	2	3
y						

2. $y = 2 - x$

x	⁻2	⁻1	0	1	2	3
y						

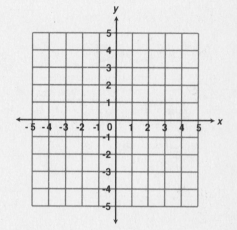

3. $y = 2x$

x	⁻2	⁻1	0	1	2
y					

4. $y = x - 2$

x	4	2	1	0	⁻1	⁻2
y						

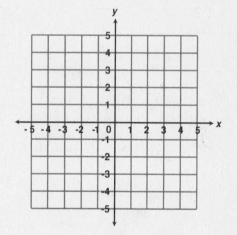

5. $y = x + 4$

x	1	0	⁻1	⁻2	⁻3	⁻4
y						

6. $y = {}^{-}1x$

x	⁻3	⁻2	⁻1	1	2	3
y						

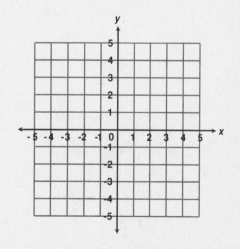

Name _____

Using the Strategies

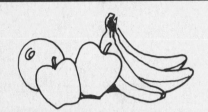

LUNCH

Juices $0.35	**Sandwiches** $1.49	**Snacks** $0.45
Orange	Tuna	Apple
Tomato	Turkey	Banana
Apple	Egg Salad	Grapes
	Burger	Yogurt
	Peanut Butter	

Use the cafeteria menu to answer the questions.

1. If a lunch consists of one juice, one sandwich, and one snack, how many different meals are possible? _____

2. If you have only juice and a sandwich, how many possibilities are there? _____

3. If you choose two different juices and a sandwich, how many choices do you have? _____

4. Suppose, as in Question 3, you choose two juices and a sandwich, but can select two cups of the same juice. How many choices do you have? _____

5. If you select only three snacks, regardless of whether they are the same, how many different choices do you have? _____

6. If you choose 3 snacks, all of which must be the same, how many choices do you have? _____

7. What is the least amount that any meal described in Questions 1–6 can cost?

   _____

8. From the meals described in Questions 1–6, what different amounts of money can you spend? _____

   _____

Name _____

Factors and Multiples

Write whether the first number is a factor of the
second.

1. 2, 20   **2.** 6, 86   **3.** 4, 86

_____   _____   _____

4. 19, 76   **5.** 11, 111   **6.** 7, 777

_____   _____   _____

List all of the factors of each number.

7. 12   **8.** 20   **9.** 10

_____   _____   _____

10. 50   **11.** 81   **12.** 66

_____   _____   _____

_____   _____   _____

List the first five nonzero multiples of each number.

13. 5   **14.** 2   **15.** 14

_____   _____   _____

16. 100   **17.** 9   **18.** 17

_____   _____   _____

_____   _____   _____

List all the factors of each number. Then list the first
four nonzero multiples of each.

19. 18   **20.** 32

Factors: _____   Factors: _____

Nonzero multiples: Nonzero multiples:

_____   _____

Divisibility

Write whether each number is divisible by 2 or 5.

1. 45   **2.** 361   **3.** 20

_____   _____   _____

4. 905   **5.** 48   **6.** 104

_____   _____   _____

Write whether each number is divisible by 3.

7. 67   **8.** 727   **9.** 396

_____   _____   _____

10. 759   **11.** 4,530   **12.** 7,623

_____   _____   _____

A number is divisible by 6 if it is divisible by both 2 and 3. Write whether each number is divisible by 6.

13. 102   **14.** 570   **15.** 428

_____   _____   _____

16. 222   **17.** 623   **18.** 366

_____   _____   _____

A number is divisible by 4 if the number formed by the last 2 digits is divisible by 4. Write whether each number is divisible by 4.

19. 348   **20.** 1,956   **21.** 21,537

_____   _____   _____

22. 739,624   **23.** 85,254   **24.** 420,441

_____   _____   _____

Name _____

Primes and Composites

Complete the table.

	Whole Number	List of All Factors	Prime or Composite?
1.	65		
2.	81		
3.	79		
4.	93		
5.	14		
6.	42		
7.	33		
8.	97		
9.	57		
10.	22		
11.	61		
12.	54		
13.	35		
14.	51		
15.	23		
16.	69		
17.	77		
18.	59		
19.	99		
20.	83		

Name _____

Using Critical Thinking

1. Enter 3 on your calculator. Divide it by 4. Add 3 to the result, and divide by 4 again. Keep doing this until something interesting happens. Describe what happens.

0.75
3.75
0.9375
3.9375
0.984375

(Keep going.)

_____

_____

_____

_____

2. Enter 1 on your calculator. Divide by 8. Continue dividing by 8 until the calculator gives a strange answer. What happens?

_____

_____

3. Enter 1 on your calculator and divide by 64. What do you think will happen if you continue to divide by 64? Try it.

_____

_____

4. Enter 1 on your calculator and divide by 128. What do you think will happen if you continue to divide by 128? Try it.

_____

_____

5. What do Exercises 2, 3, and 4 have in common?

_____

_____

Name _____

Prime Factorization

Use factor trees to find the prime factorization of each number.

1. 18

2. 56

3. 88

_____   _____   _____

4. 126

5. 198

6. 260

_____   _____   _____

Use repeated division to find the prime factorization of each number.

7. 65

8. 70

9. 100

_____   _____   _____

10. 242

11. 315

12. 545

_____   _____   _____

Solve each equation to find the number whose prime factorization is given.

13. $n = 2^4 \cdot 5$

14. $n = 2 \cdot 3 \cdot 5 \cdot 7$

15. $n = 2 \cdot 3^2 \cdot 11$

_____   _____   _____

16. $n = 5^3 \cdot 7$

17. $n = 7^2 \cdot 13$

18. $n = 2^2 \cdot 3^2 \cdot 5^2$

_____   _____   _____

Using the Strategies

Solve.

1. A board $14\frac{3}{4}$ in. long is cut from a board $36\frac{1}{4}$ in. long. The saw cut takes $\frac{1}{8}$ in. How long is the piece of board that is left?

_____

2. Boards for shelves cost $2.64 each. Brackets for shelves cost $0.88 each. What is the total cost of 3 shelves and 6 brackets?

_____

3. Zelda wants to cut a 40-in.-long board to get 3 pieces each $12\frac{1}{2}$ in. long. If each saw cut takes $\frac{1}{8}$ in., how many inches of board will be left?

_____

4. A sheet of paneling is 4 ft wide. Raul used a piece $2\frac{3}{4}$ ft wide. How wide was the piece he had left?

_____

5. A 12 d nail is $3\frac{1}{4}$ in. long. A 4 d nail is $1\frac{1}{2}$ in. How much longer is the 12 d nail than the 4 d nail?

_____

6. Sarah is nailing together two boards each $1\frac{5}{8}$ in. wide. What will be the total width?

_____

7. A repairman charged $12.50 an hour plus $48.35 for parts. What was the total bill for $4\frac{1}{2}$ hours of work?

_____

8. A hole is drilled $2\frac{3}{8}$ in. from each end of a 14-in. board. What is the distance between the holes?

_____

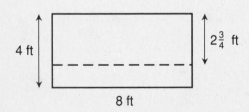

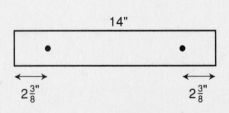

Greatest Common Factor

List the factors of each number. Then give the greatest common factor (GCF) of each pair of numbers.

1. 8: _____

12: _____ GCF: __

2. 16: _____

20: _____ GCF: __

3. 24: _____

36: _____

_____ GCF: __

4. 40: _____

60: _____

_____ GCF: __

Use prime factorizations to find the GCF of each pair of numbers.

5. 12 = _____

9 = _____ GCF: __

6. 45 = _____

36 = _____ GCF: _____

7. 24 = _____

40 = _____ GCF: _____

8. 15 = _____

30 = _____ GCF: _____

9. 50 = _____

75 = _____ GCF: _____

10. 20 = _____

90 = _____ GCF: _____

11. 32 = _____

48 = _____ GCF: _____

12. 21 = _____

25 = _____ GCF: _____

13. 90 = _____

120 = _____ GCF: _____

14. 12 = _____

28 = _____ GCF: _____

15. 52 = _____

60 = _____ GCF: _____

16. 17 = _____

12 = _____ GCF: _____

17. 34 = _____

51 = _____ GCF: _____

18. 42 = _____

63 = _____ GCF: _____

Least Common Multiple

Find the least common multiple (LCM) of each group
of numbers.

1. 9 and 12 _____   **2.** 4 and 10 _____   **3.** 2 and 7 _____

4. 10 and 6 _____   **5.** 15 and 12 _____   **6.** 9 and 21 _____

7. 5 and 8 _____   **8.** 9 and 4 _____   **9.** 6 and 15 _____

10. 8, 6, and 12 _____   **11.** 6, 9, and 12 _____   **12.** 3, 4, and 5 _____

13. 2, 4, and 6 _____   **14.** 5, 8, and 20 _____   **15.** 2, 3, and 9 _____

Use prime factorizations to find the LCM of each
pair.

16. 3, 4 _____   **17.** 2, 5 _____

18. 9, 6 _____   **19.** 4, 6 _____

20. 10, 4 _____   **21.** 7, 2 _____

22. 3, 5 _____   **23.** 8, 6 _____

24. 12, 9 _____   **25.** 8, 12 _____

26. 4, 5 _____   **27.** 8, 10 _____

28. 2, 11 _____   **29.** 12, 10 _____

30. 9, 4 _____   **31.** 10, 15 _____

Name _____

Exploring Algebra: Functions with Exponents

Complete the tables by using your calculator to
evaluate each expression.

1.

x	$y = 3x^2 - 7$
$^-6$	
$^-3$	
0	
1.5	
5	
2.1	

2.

x	$y = 8x^2 - 22$
$^-3$	
$^-1.7$	
0	
1.7	
3	
$^-3.2$	

3.

x	$y = {}^-4x^2 + 32$
$^-5$	
0	
1	
2.8	
5.4	
$^-5.4$	

4.

x	$y = {}^-1x^2 + 1$
$^-4.4$	
$^-1$	
0	
1	
3.3	
$^-3.3$	

5.

x	$y = x^3 + x$
$^-3$	
$^-2$	
0.5	
1	
7	
$^-7$	
1.5	

6.

x	$y = 10x^2 + 10x + 10$
$^-8$	
$^-4$	
0	
1	
5	
$^-5$	
2.5	

Name _____

Problem Solving Checklist

Solve. What data are extra?

1. The average American uses 60 gallons of water per
   day in the home. Approximately 41% of the water
   used is for flushing toilets. Another 37% is used
   for washing and bathing. What percent of the
   water is not used for washing, bathing, or flushing?

2. There are over 90 million motor vehicles in
   America today. They produce around 92 million
   tons of air pollution per year. If the total production
   of air pollution per year is 191 million tons, about
   what percentage is contributed by motor vehicles?

3. The U.S. population in 1970 was approximately
   207,000,000. By the year 2030 it is estimated that
   the population of 1970 will be doubled. In 1910
   the population was about half of the 1970
   population. How many people will there be in the
   United States in 2030?

4. There are $7\frac{1}{2}$ gallons of water in a cubic foot. A
   cubic foot of water weighs $62\frac{1}{2}$ pounds. The
   average American uses 60 gallons of water per day.
   How much does a gallon of water weigh?

5. If you had to carry the water that the average
   American uses in the home each day for 3 miles,
   how many pounds of water would you have to
   carry? (Use 8.33 pounds per gallon of water.)

Fractions

Write the missing fractions.

1. $\dfrac{3}{5} = \dfrac{3 \times 4}{5 \times 4} =$ _____

2. $\dfrac{1}{6} = \dfrac{1 \times 5}{6 \times 5} =$ _____

3. $\dfrac{5}{8} = \dfrac{5 \times 3}{8 \times 3} =$ _____

4. $\dfrac{5}{12} = \dfrac{5 \times 2}{12 \times 2} =$ _____

5. $\dfrac{3}{4} = \dfrac{3 \times 6}{4 \times 6} =$ _____

6. $\dfrac{7}{10} = \dfrac{7 \times 4}{10 \times 4} =$ _____

7. $\dfrac{2}{15} = \dfrac{2 \times 3}{15 \times 3} =$ _____

8. $\dfrac{2}{3} = \dfrac{2 \times 7}{3 \times 7} =$ _____

9. $\dfrac{5}{4} = \dfrac{5 \times 2}{4 \times 2} =$ _____

Express each fraction as a mixed number or fraction
in lowest terms.

10. $\dfrac{10}{40} =$ _____

11. $\dfrac{15}{18} =$ _____

12. $\dfrac{6}{15} =$ _____

13. $\dfrac{8}{12} =$ _____

14. $\dfrac{10}{24} =$ _____

15. $\dfrac{22}{16} =$ _____

16. $\dfrac{20}{32} =$ _____

17. $\dfrac{16}{20} =$ _____

18. $\dfrac{25}{60} =$ _____

19. $\dfrac{6}{18} =$ _____

20. $\dfrac{25}{15} =$ _____

21. $\dfrac{30}{25} =$ _____

Write = or ≠ for each ◯ .

22. $\dfrac{15}{18}$ ◯ $\dfrac{35}{42}$

23. $\dfrac{10}{25}$ ◯ $\dfrac{18}{45}$

24. $\dfrac{21}{24}$ ◯ $\dfrac{3}{4}$

25. $\dfrac{6}{15}$ ◯ $\dfrac{12}{30}$

26. $\dfrac{3}{5}$ ◯ $\dfrac{42}{70}$

27. $\dfrac{6}{21}$ ◯ $\dfrac{8}{24}$

28. $\dfrac{9}{24}$ ◯ $\dfrac{27}{72}$

29. $\dfrac{12}{32}$ ◯ $\dfrac{16}{40}$

30. $\dfrac{8}{20}$ ◯ $\dfrac{18}{45}$

31. $\dfrac{14}{21}$ ◯ $\dfrac{24}{64}$

32. $\dfrac{24}{30}$ ◯ $\dfrac{15}{32}$

33. $\dfrac{6}{21}$ ◯ $\dfrac{10}{35}$

Name _____

Rational Numbers and the Number Line

Write, in fractional form, a rational number that
corresponds to the given point. If appropriate, write
the fraction as a mixed number.

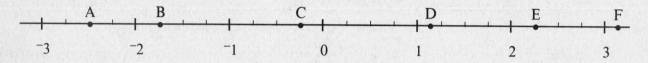

1. A _____

2. B _____

3. C _____

4. D _____

5. E _____

6. F _____

Write the opposite of each in 3 different ways.

7. $\frac{4}{5}$ _____

8. $\frac{3}{4}$ _____

9. $\frac{2}{7}$ _____

10. $\frac{1}{3}$ _____

11. $\frac{7}{15}$ _____

12. $\frac{2}{3}$ _____

Write the opposite of each of these rational numbers.

13. $\frac{1}{3}$ _____

14. $\frac{3}{5}$ _____

15. $\frac{^-3}{4}$ _____

16. $\frac{4}{5}$ _____

17. $-\frac{2}{5}$ _____

18. 0 _____

19. $\frac{7}{^-10}$ _____

20. $\frac{^-4}{5}$ _____

21. $\frac{3}{^-5}$ _____

Name _____

Comparing and Ordering Rational Numbers

Compare. Use < or >.

1. $\frac{1}{2} \bigcirc \frac{3}{8}$ 2. $\frac{1}{4} \bigcirc \frac{1}{3}$ 3. $\frac{2}{3} \bigcirc \frac{3}{5}$ 4. $\frac{1}{7} \bigcirc \frac{1}{8}$

5. $\frac{3}{4} \bigcirc \frac{7}{10}$ 6. $\frac{1}{4} \bigcirc \frac{1}{2}$ 7. $\frac{1}{4} \bigcirc \frac{5}{16}$ 8. $\frac{6}{10} \bigcirc \frac{2}{3}$

9. $\frac{5}{7} \bigcirc \frac{3}{4}$ 10. $\frac{6}{7} \bigcirc \frac{5}{6}$ 11 $\frac{1}{2} \bigcirc \frac{1}{6}$ 12. $\frac{1}{4} \bigcirc \frac{1}{5}$

13. $\frac{5}{6} \bigcirc \frac{7}{10}$ 14. $\frac{3}{4} \bigcirc \frac{2}{3}$ 15. $\frac{3}{4} \bigcirc \frac{7}{8}$ 16. $\frac{5}{8} \bigcirc \frac{1}{2}$

Compare. Use < or >.

17. $4\frac{2}{3} \bigcirc 4\frac{5}{8}$ 18. $2.8 \bigcirc 3.83$ 19. $5\frac{11}{12} \bigcirc 5\frac{9}{10}$ 20. $7\frac{3}{4} \bigcirc 7\frac{5}{6}$

21. $3\frac{1}{2} \bigcirc 3\frac{3}{5}$ 22. $10\frac{3}{8} \bigcirc 10\frac{2}{3}$ 23. $6.9 \bigcirc 6.875$ 24. $11\frac{7}{8} \bigcirc 11\frac{5}{6}$

25. $9\frac{4}{10} \bigcirc 9\frac{1}{2}$ 26. $1\frac{3}{8} \bigcirc 1\frac{1}{4}$ 27. $4\frac{2}{3} \bigcirc 5\frac{5}{6}$ 28. $8.375 \bigcirc 8.75$

29. $14.5 \bigcirc 14\frac{2}{5}$ 30. $3.6 \bigcirc 3\frac{14}{20}$ 31. $7.25 \bigcirc 7\frac{3}{16}$ 32. $2\frac{6}{10} \bigcirc 2\frac{1}{2}$

Arrange each list of numbers in order from smallest to largest.

33. $\frac{1}{4}, \frac{1}{6}, \frac{1}{8}$ _____   34. $\frac{5}{7}, \frac{7}{8}, \frac{5}{6}$ _____

35. $1\frac{5}{9}, 1\frac{2}{3}, 1\frac{4}{5}$ _____   36. $2\frac{9}{16}, 2\frac{3}{4}, 2\frac{5}{8}$ _____

Name _____

Rational Numbers as Decimals

Write a decimal for each fraction. Use a bar to show
repeating decimals.

1. $\frac{3}{4} =$ _____   2. $\frac{2}{3} =$ _____

3. $\frac{5}{8} =$ _____   4. $\frac{5}{11} =$ _____

5. $\frac{14}{50} =$ _____   6. $\frac{8}{9} =$ _____

7. $\frac{1}{15} =$ _____   8. $\frac{5}{6} =$ _____

9. $\frac{7}{2} =$ _____   10. $\frac{11}{8} =$ _____

11. $\frac{3}{5} =$ _____   12. $\frac{32}{99} =$ _____

13. $\frac{1}{8} =$ _____   14. $\frac{7}{15} =$ _____

15. $\frac{17}{4} =$ _____   16. $\frac{4}{9} =$ _____

17. $\frac{7}{16} =$ _____   18. $\frac{1}{6} =$ _____

19. $\frac{9}{8} =$ _____   20. $\frac{8}{25} =$ _____

21. $\frac{4}{3} =$ _____   22. $\frac{27}{50} =$ _____

23. $\frac{17}{22} =$ _____   24. $\frac{7}{5} =$ _____

25. $\frac{16}{11} =$ _____   26. $\frac{31}{8} =$ _____

27. $\frac{5}{12} =$ _____   28. $\frac{66}{100} =$ _____

29. $\frac{9}{22} =$ _____   30. $\frac{11}{9} =$ _____

Name _____

Adding and Subtracting Fractions

Find the sums. Express your answer in lowest terms.

1. $\dfrac{9}{10} + \dfrac{^-3}{10} =$ _____

2. $\dfrac{^-5}{6} + \dfrac{1}{6} =$ _____

3. $\dfrac{^-2}{7} + \dfrac{^-3}{7} =$ _____

4. $\dfrac{^-5}{8} + \dfrac{1}{8} =$ _____

5. $\dfrac{1}{2} + \dfrac{^-5}{2} =$ _____

6. $\dfrac{^-5}{12} + \dfrac{7}{12} =$ _____

7. $\dfrac{2}{3} + \dfrac{^-1}{2} =$ _____

8. $\dfrac{^-1}{8} + \dfrac{^-1}{4} =$ _____

9. $\dfrac{^-3}{10} + \dfrac{^-31}{100} =$ _____

10. $\dfrac{^-1}{3} + \dfrac{5}{12} =$ _____

11. $1\dfrac{1}{2} + {^-2}\dfrac{1}{4} =$ _____

12. $6 + {^-4}\dfrac{3}{4} =$ _____

13. $^-2.1 + 3.5 =$ _____

14. $6.0 - 5.8 =$ _____

15. $-0.8 + -0.3 =$ _____

16. $0.5 + -2.0 =$ _____

Find the differences. Express your answer in lowest terms.

17. $\dfrac{^-3}{5} - \dfrac{4}{5} =$ _____

18. $\dfrac{^-1}{2} - \dfrac{1}{2} =$ _____

19. $\dfrac{13}{16} - \dfrac{9}{16} =$ _____

20. $\dfrac{^-4}{7} - \dfrac{^-5}{7} =$ _____

21. $\dfrac{^-3}{20} - \dfrac{^-11}{20} =$ _____

22. $\dfrac{1}{3} - \dfrac{^-5}{3} =$ _____

23. $\dfrac{1}{4} - \dfrac{^-1}{2} =$ _____

24. $\dfrac{^-2}{3} - \dfrac{1}{4} =$ _____

25. $\dfrac{^-5}{8} - \dfrac{^-7}{12} =$ _____

26. $\dfrac{5}{6} - \dfrac{^-2}{15} =$ _____

27. $5\dfrac{1}{2} - 6 =$ _____

28. $^-1\dfrac{2}{3} - \dfrac{^-2}{3} =$ _____

29. $0.4 - {^-0.2} =$ _____

30. $1.0 - 2.7 =$ _____

Name _____

Adding and Subtracting Mixed Numbers

Add or subtract.

1. $7\frac{1}{2}$

$-2\frac{3}{4}$

2. $8\frac{1}{3}$

$-1\frac{5}{6}$

3. $9\frac{5}{8}$

$+2\frac{3}{4}$

4. 12

$-4\frac{1}{2}$

5. $6\frac{1}{4}$

$-2\frac{3}{8}$

6. $32\frac{1}{8}$

$+14\frac{1}{2}$

7. $46\frac{3}{10}$

$-15\frac{1}{2}$

8. $25\frac{1}{3}$

$-16\frac{7}{8}$

9. $39\frac{2}{3}$

$+31\frac{4}{5}$

10. 63

$-27\frac{5}{7}$

11. $12\frac{1}{4}$

$+9\frac{5}{16}$

12. 42

$-27\frac{3}{11}$

13. $34\frac{2}{9}$

$+24\frac{5}{6}$

14. 66

$-19\frac{5}{24}$

Name _____

Using Critical Thinking

Try the number tricks below. Then write the steps to
show why each one works.

1. Choose a number. Multiply it by 5.
Add 4 to the result. Multiply by 2.
Subtract 8. Divide by 10. The answer
should be your number.

2. Choose a number. Add 4 to it. Multiply
the result by 6. Subtract 10 from that
number. Then subtract 14. Divide that
number by 6. The answer should be
your number.

3. Take your age. Add 10 to it. Multiply
the result by 7. Then subtract 14.
Divide that result by 7. Subtract 8.
The answer should be your age.

4. Choose a number. Double it. Then
triple that number. Add 14 to your
result. Multiply that number by 2 and
then subtract 12. Take that number
and subtract 16. Divide that number
by your original number. The answer
should be 12.

Name _____

Multiplying Rational Numbers

Find the products. Express the answer as a mixed
number or fraction in lowest terms.

1. $\dfrac{1}{3} \cdot \dfrac{^-3}{4} =$ _____

2. $25 \cdot \dfrac{^-1}{8} =$ _____

3. $\dfrac{9}{10} \cdot \dfrac{^-1}{3} =$ _____

4. $\dfrac{^-2}{5} \cdot \dfrac{^-3}{2} =$ _____

5. $\dfrac{^-5}{2} \cdot {^-2} =$ _____

6. $\dfrac{^-2}{3} \cdot \dfrac{^-2}{3} =$ _____

7. $\dfrac{4}{9} \cdot \dfrac{3}{2} =$ _____

8. $\dfrac{^-3}{4} \cdot 16 =$ _____

9. $\dfrac{^-3}{8} \cdot \dfrac{^-8}{3} =$ _____

10. $30 \cdot \dfrac{^-7}{9} =$ _____

11. $2\dfrac{1}{3} \cdot {^-3} =$ _____

12. $^-5 \cdot 1\dfrac{4}{5} =$ _____

13. $\dfrac{^-7}{10} \cdot \dfrac{4}{5} =$ _____

14. $\dfrac{^-3}{5} \cdot \dfrac{^-7}{10} =$ _____

15. $\dfrac{1}{8} \cdot \dfrac{^-3}{4} =$ _____

16. $\dfrac{^-9}{10} \cdot \dfrac{^-1}{5} =$ _____

17. $\dfrac{5}{2} \cdot \dfrac{^-3}{4} =$ _____

18. $\dfrac{^-1}{4} \cdot \dfrac{^-1}{2} =$ _____

19. $2 \cdot \dfrac{^-1}{3} =$ _____

20. $\dfrac{^-3}{5} \cdot \dfrac{1}{10} =$ _____

21. $\dfrac{10}{11} \cdot \dfrac{^-2}{11} =$ _____

22. $\dfrac{^-5}{6} \cdot \dfrac{^-5}{8} =$ _____

23. $^-6 \cdot 2\dfrac{1}{4} =$ _____

24. $10\dfrac{1}{2} \cdot \dfrac{^-5}{8} =$ _____

Exploring Algebra: Reciprocals and Negative Exponents

Write the reciprocal of each number.

1. $\dfrac{1}{4}$

2. $\dfrac{2}{7}$

3. 9

_____

_____

_____

4. $3\dfrac{1}{2}$

5. 5^8

6. 10^4

_____

_____

_____

7. 8^2

8. 10^{-7}

9. 1^{-1}

_____

_____

_____

Simplify. Write the expression with positive exponents.

10. $\dfrac{2^6}{2^4}$

11. $\dfrac{10^9}{10^5}$

12. $\dfrac{7^5}{7^{11}}$

_____

_____

_____

13. $\dfrac{3^3 \cdot 3^5}{3^{10}}$

14. $\dfrac{5^{12}}{5^4 \cdot 5^6}$

15. $(^-7)^5 \cdot (^-7)^1$

_____

_____

_____

16. $6^8 \cdot 6^{-6}$

17. $10^3 \cdot 10^{-8}$

18. $\dfrac{a^8}{a^3}$

_____

_____

_____

19. $\dfrac{x^5}{x^8}$

20. $\dfrac{x^{-3}}{x^4}$

21. $x^5 \cdot x^{-2}$

_____

_____

_____

22. $\dfrac{y^4}{y^{-8}}$

23. $\dfrac{y^5}{y^{-9}}$

24. $\dfrac{y^8}{y^{-8}}$

_____

_____

_____

Name _____

Dividing Rational Numbers

Find these quotients. Express as a fraction or mixed number in lowest terms.

1. $2\frac{1}{3} \div 2\frac{1}{3}$ _____

2. $1\frac{1}{4} \div 2\frac{1}{2} =$ _____

3. $3\frac{5}{8} \div {}^-1\frac{1}{4} =$ _____

4. $2\frac{1}{4} \div 1\frac{1}{8} =$ _____

5. $2\frac{1}{4} \div 3 =$ _____

6. ${}^-4\frac{1}{6} \div {}^-1\frac{2}{3} =$ _____

7. $1\frac{1}{2} \div 3 =$ _____

8. $2\frac{7}{8} \div 1\frac{1}{8} =$ _____

9. $2\frac{4}{5} \div 2\frac{1}{3} =$ _____

10. ${}^-5 \div 1\frac{{}^-1}{4} =$ _____

11. $1 \div 4 =$ _____

12. ${}^-2 \div 1\frac{1}{5} =$ _____

13. $3\frac{1}{3} \div 1\frac{2}{3} =$ _____

14. $2\frac{3}{4} \div 2\frac{1}{2} =$ _____

15. $12 \div \frac{3}{4} =$ _____

16. ${}^-15 \div \frac{5}{6} =$ _____

17. $3\frac{1}{2} \div 1\frac{2}{5} =$ _____

18. ${}^-2\frac{1}{3} \div \frac{{}^-7}{9} =$ _____

19. $6\frac{3}{4} \div {}^-3 =$ _____

20. $14 \div 1\frac{1}{2} =$ _____

21. $3\frac{1}{2} \div 1\frac{1}{2} =$ _____

Perform these operations.

22. $\left({}^-2\frac{1}{3} + 1\frac{1}{6}\right) \div 7 =$ _____

23. $\left(3\frac{1}{2} - 2\frac{3}{4}\right) \div \frac{{}^-1}{8} =$ _____

24. $\frac{{}^-1}{3} \times \left(5 \div \frac{5}{8}\right) =$ _____

25. $\left(\frac{2}{3} \div \frac{4}{9}\right) \times 1\frac{1}{3} =$ _____

26. $\left(8 - {}^-3\frac{3}{4}\right) \div 3\frac{1}{4} =$ _____

27. $\left(2\frac{1}{4} + 1\frac{1}{8}\right) \div {}^-1\frac{1}{8} =$ _____

Name _____

Using the Strategies

Solve. Use any problem solving strategy.

1. The population of the United Kingdom is 56.9 million. The population of the Netherlands is about $\frac{8}{31}$ as much. What is the approximate population of the Netherlands?

   _____

2. A dealer sold 16 cars in the first week last month, 22 cars in the second week, and 21 cars in the third week. How many cars did he sell in the fourth week if the average of all 4 weeks is 25 cars?

   _____

3. A phonograph record turns 45 times per minute. How many times would that record turn playing a song that is $2\frac{3}{5}$ minutes long?

   _____

4. It took 5 strips of wallpaper, each 71 cm wide, and one strip 42 cm wide to cover a wall of a room. What was the width of the wall covered by the wallpaper?

   _____

5. Helene rode her bicycle for $3\frac{1}{3}$ hours. Her rate of travel was about $6\frac{1}{2}$ miles per hour. How far did she ride?

   _____

6. The distance between Independence and Fort Laramie, Missouri, is about 1,000 km. Driving at 80 km per hour, how long would it take to drive the distance?

   _____

7. Tauna plays the flute. She practices $\frac{3}{4}$ hour every weekday and $1\frac{1}{2}$ hours on both Saturday and Sunday. How many hours does she practice each week?

   _____

8. It takes 17 trees to make one ton of paper. Americans use 50 million tons of paper each year. How many trees are used to make paper each year?

   _____

Scientific Notation

Write in standard form.

1. 3.7×10^5 _____

2. 6.85×10^4 _____

3. 9.2×10^8 _____

4. 5.03×10^6 _____

5. 8×10^{10} _____

6. 7.14×10^{-7} _____

7. 1.91×10^2 _____

8. 6.38×10^9 _____

9. 9×10^{11} _____

10. 4.04×10^{-3} _____

11. 18×10^1 _____

12. 2.23×10^{-5} _____

13. 9.6×10^4 _____

14. 3.7×10^6 _____

Write in scientific notation.

15. 41,000,000 _____

16. 0.720 _____

17. 163,000,000,000 _____

18. 9,000 _____

19. 2,800,000,000,000,000 _____

20. 33,000,000,000,000 _____

21. 470,000,000 _____

22. 2,090,000,000 _____

23. 7,000,000,000 _____

24. 60,000 _____

25. 860,000 _____

26. 1,000,000,000,000 _____

27. 73,000,000,000 _____

28. 6,500,000 _____

Name _____

Finding Related Problems

Mr. Singh manufactures electronic equipment. He wants to have copies made of his user's manuals and advertising brochures. Use the price chart to solve these problems.

Number of Copies

Number of Pages	1–3	4–10	11–25	51–99	100+
1–3	$0.25	$0.15	$0.095	$0.08	$0.07
4–10	0.15	0.095	0.09	0.075	0.065
11–20	0.095	0.09	0.08	0.07	0.06
21–35	0.09	0.08	0.075	0.065	0.055
36–49	0.08	0.075	0.07	0.06	0.055
50–99	0.075	0.07	0.065	0.0575	0.0525
100–299	0.07	0.065	0.06	0.055	0.05
300+	0.065	0.06	0.0575	0.0525	0.0475

Cost per Page

1. How much will it cost Mr. Singh to make 75 copies of a technical manual with 62 pages?

_____

2. Mr. Singh wants to make 25 copies each of 4 brochures. One brochure has 8 pages, one has 16 pages, one has 6 pages, and one has 2 pages. What will be the total cost if he has each brochure copied separately?

_____

3. How much would the 4 brochures in Problem 2 cost if Mr. Singh combined all the pages?

_____

4. Would it be cheaper for Mr. Singh to copy the brochures separately or to combine them? How much cheaper?

_____

5. How much would it cost to make 150 copies of a 320-page technical manual and 100 copies of a 1-page advertising flyer?

_____

6. What is the average (mean) cost per page for 51–99 copies?

_____

7. What is the mean cost per page for 50–99 pages?

_____

Name _____

Ratio and Proportion

Write each ratio in two other ways.

1. 7 to 9 _____ **2.** 4:7 _____

3. $\dfrac{2}{3}$ _____ **4.** 8:5 _____

5. 10 to 13 _____ **6.** 15:18 _____

7. $\dfrac{1}{50}$ _____ **8.** 9:14 _____

9. 70 to 81 _____ **10.** 6:1 _____

Write the next three ratios in each pattern.

11. $\dfrac{2}{5} = \dfrac{4}{10} = \dfrac{6}{15} = \underline{\ \ } = \underline{\ \ } = \underline{\ \ }$ **12.** 2:9, 4:18, 6:27, _____, _____,

_____

13. 4:1, 8:2, 12:3, _____, _____, _____ **14.** 6:5, 12:10, 18:15, _____, _____,

_____

15. $\dfrac{5}{8} = \dfrac{10}{16} = \dfrac{15}{24} = \underline{\ \ } = \underline{\ \ } = \underline{\ \ }$ **16.** $\dfrac{42}{54} = \dfrac{35}{45} = \dfrac{28}{36} = \underline{\ \ } = \underline{\ \ } = \underline{\ \ }$

Compare these ratios in fraction form. Use > or <.

17. 1 to 5 and 2 to 15 **18.** 4 to 7 and 5 to 8

_____ _____

19. 7 to 14 and 5 to 12 **20.** 3 to 8 and 1 to 5

_____ _____

Name _____

Rate

Simplify each rate. Either complete a table or do the division in one step.

1. $\dfrac{95 \text{ cm}}{5 \text{ s}}$ _____

2. $\dfrac{48 \text{ km}}{4 \text{ L}}$ _____

3. $\dfrac{\$78}{6 \text{ hr}}$ _____

4. $\dfrac{400 \text{ km}}{8 \text{ hr}}$ _____

5. $\dfrac{\$3.69}{9 \text{ L}}$ _____

6. $\dfrac{196 \text{ people}}{7 \text{ boats}}$ _____

7. $\dfrac{170 \text{ people}}{5 \text{ buses}}$ _____

8. $\dfrac{84 \text{ students}}{4 \text{ teachers}}$ _____

9. $\dfrac{\$30}{4 \text{ hr}}$ _____

10. $\dfrac{28 \text{ problems}}{20 \text{ minutes}}$ _____

11. $\dfrac{180 \text{ revolutions}}{4 \text{ minutes}}$ _____

12. $\dfrac{56 \text{ pages}}{40 \text{ minutes}}$ _____

13. $\dfrac{\$18}{2 \text{ hours}}$ _____

14. $\dfrac{60 \text{ m}}{24 \text{ sec}}$ _____

15. Ann charged $7.50 for 3 hours of gardening. What is her hourly rate?

18. Henry typed 486 words in 6 minutes. What is his typing rate in words per minute?

16. Carlos drove 160 km in 2.5 hours. How many kilometers did he travel per hour?

19. Terry picked 44 apples in 8 minutes. At what rate did Terry pick the apples?

17. Kara read 45 pages in 60 minutes. What is her reading rate in pages per minute?

20. Virginia charged $18.75 for 5 hours of housecleaning. What was her rate?

Unit Pricing

Find the unit price. Use a calculator if possible.

1.

Unit price	
London broil 1.35 kg for $10.80	

2.

Unit price	
Apples 2.2 kg for $4.96	

3.

Unit price	
Green beans 5 cans for $2.05	

4.

Unit price	
Carrots 1.5 kg for $3.30	

5.

Unit price	
Olive oil 0.7 L for $3.92	

6.

Unit price	
Raisins 0.8 kg for $3.52	

7.

Unit price	
Molasses 0.35 L for $1.26	

8.

Unit price	
Walnuts 0.65 kg for $3.52	

9.

Unit price	
Cheddar cheese 1.25 kg for $5.75	

10.

Unit price	
Bananas 0.45 kg for $0.99	

11.

Unit price	
Ham 2.6 kg for $9.88	

12.

Unit price	
Tomatoes 1.7 kg for $1.87	

Find the unit price of each item. Which choice has the lower unit price?

13. Strawberries

    A 2 baskets for $0.89 _____/basket

    B 3 baskets for $1.37 _____/basket

14. Tomato sauce

    A 5 cans for $1.00 _____/can

    B 3 cans for $0.67 _____/can

15. Cheese

    A 0.45 kg for $1.35 _____/kg

    B 0.6 kg for $1.92 _____/kg

16. Paper towels

    A 3 rolls for $2.37 _____/roll

    B 2 rolls for $1.38 _____/roll

17. Mushrooms

    A 0.45 kg for $0.99 _____/kg

    B 0.75 kg for $1.71 _____/kg

18. Chicken

    A 1.85 kg for $3.33_____/kg

    B 1.4 kg for $2.31 _____/kg

Name _____

Solving Proportions

Solve each proportion. Use cross products.

1. $\dfrac{5}{6}=\dfrac{f}{12}$

_____

_____

2. $\dfrac{u}{40}=\dfrac{7}{8}$

_____

_____

3. $\dfrac{7}{g}=\dfrac{1}{4}$

_____

_____

4. $\dfrac{x}{18}=\dfrac{2}{3}$

_____

_____

5. $\dfrac{d}{40}=\dfrac{8}{12}$

_____

_____

6. $\dfrac{8}{t}=\dfrac{24}{30}$

_____

_____

7. $\dfrac{30}{k}=\dfrac{15}{18}$

_____

_____

8. $\dfrac{3}{6}=\dfrac{8}{m}$

_____

_____

9. $\dfrac{14}{35}=\dfrac{b}{20}$

_____

_____

10. $\dfrac{4}{5}=\dfrac{s}{25}$

_____

_____

11. $\dfrac{9}{12}=\dfrac{10}{a}$

_____

_____

12. $\dfrac{h}{24}=\dfrac{6}{8}$

_____

_____

13. $\dfrac{3}{c}=\dfrac{7}{35}$

_____

_____

14. $\dfrac{9}{12}=\dfrac{15}{y}$

_____

_____

15. $\dfrac{4}{6}=\dfrac{n}{20}$

_____

_____

16. $\dfrac{y}{50}=\dfrac{12}{30}$

_____

_____

17. $\dfrac{q}{72}=\dfrac{7}{8}$

_____

_____

18. $\dfrac{7}{21}=\dfrac{8}{e}$

_____

_____

Name _____

Scale and Proportions

A map of Colorado has a scale of 1 cm = 75 km.
Find the air distances between these cities, to the
nearest kilometer.

	Cities	Map distance	Actual air distance
1.	Denver—Grand Junction	4.2 cm	_____
2.	Denver—Colorado Springs	1.4 cm	_____
3.	Colorado Springs—Durango	4.5 cm	_____
4.	Durango—Grand Junction	3.0 cm	_____
5.	Durango—Denver	5.2 cm	_____
6.	Colorado Springs—Pueblo	0.9 cm	_____
7.	Pueblo—Grand Junction	4.9 cm	_____
8.	Denver—Pueblo	2.3 cm	_____

9. This scale drawing of a building is 3 cm long and 1.2 cm wide.

What is the actual length? _____

What is the actual width? _____

Scale: 1 cm = 10 m

10. On a scale drawing, the moon is shown about 7.7 cm from Earth. The scale is 1 cm = 50,000 km. About how many kilometers is the moon from Earth?

_____

11. Find the length of the board if the scale is 3 cm = 2 m.

_____

9 cm

12. The airline distance from London to Berlin is about 930 km. How far apart would the cities be on a map with a scale of 1 cm = 150 km?

_____

Name _____

Using the Strategies

Solve. Use any problem solving strategy.

	Luis	Alberto	Maria	Cara
hockey				
tennis				
soccer				
football				

1. Luis, Alberto, Maria, and Cara each like a different sport. Maria's brother likes hockey. Cara does not like tennis. Luis used to enjoy football, but he prefers soccer now. Which sport does each like to play?

2. The Clarks, Guzmans, Lees, and Hamas own 4 different cars: a Chevy, a Toyota, a Ford, and a Nissan. The Clarks used to own a Chevy, but they traded it for a Toyota. The Guzmans did not buy a Ford. The Lees always buy a Nissan. Which family owns which car?

_____

_____

3. Mike, John, Tara, and Michelle collected leaves for a biology project. Mike found oak leaves. His sister found maple leaves. John thought he had found birch leaves, but he had not. Michelle is John's sister. Who found elm leaves?

_____

4. The Murts have 4 pets: a cat, a dog, a pony, and a fish. Goldie weighs more than the fish or the cat. The cat is younger than Chelsea. Zippy is friendly with the pony, the fish, and the cat.

Which pet is Sam? _____

5. Larry, Robert, and Frank each collect one of the following: stamps, coins, or baseball cards. Larry does not collect anything sticky. Robert does not collect anything rectangular. Who collects

what? _____

_____

_____

_____

6. Greg's cat will not eat blueberries. His dog prefers fruits that are yellow. His lizard eats anything circular. His finch will only eat peaches. Each pet will eat only 1 of these fruits: blueberries, peaches, bananas, or apples. Which pet eats which fruit?

Tangent Ratio

Find tan A to the nearest hundredth.

1. tan A = _____

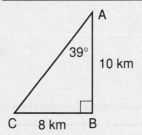

2. tan A = _____

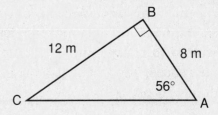

3. tan A = _____

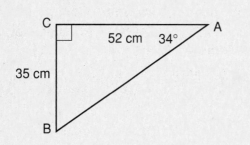

4. tan A = _____

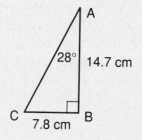

5. tan A = _____

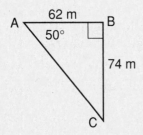

6. tan A = _____

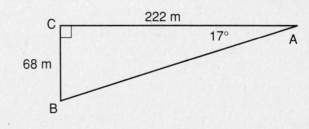

7. tan A = _____

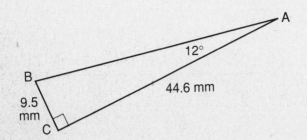

8. tan A = _____

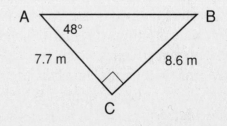

Name _____

Percent

Write a fraction, a decimal, and a percent for the part
of each region that is shaded.

1.

_____

2.

_____

3.

_____

4.

_____

5.

_____

6.

_____

Complete the table.

	Ratio	Fraction	Decimal	Percent
7.	41 for every 100			
8.	15 out of 100			
9.	48 to 100			
10.	73 per 100			
11.	96 to 100			
12.	8 for every 100			
13.	17 out of 100			

Name _____

Fractions and Percents

Write the percent for each fraction.

1. $\frac{1}{10}$ _____

2. $\frac{3}{5}$ _____

3. $\frac{23}{100}$ _____

4. $\frac{3}{20}$ _____

5. $\frac{9}{10}$ _____

6. $\frac{1}{100}$ _____

7. $\frac{33}{50}$ _____

8. $\frac{1}{4}$ _____

9. $\frac{12}{25}$ _____

10. $\frac{3}{4}$ _____

11. $\frac{1}{2}$ _____

12. $\frac{27}{50}$ _____

13. $\frac{13}{100}$ _____

14. $\frac{11}{20}$ _____

15. $\frac{4}{5}$ _____

16. $\frac{1}{3}$ _____

17. $\frac{11}{12}$ _____

18. $\frac{4}{9}$ _____

19. $\frac{11}{36}$ _____

20. $\frac{1}{6}$ _____

21. $\frac{2}{3}$ _____

22. $\frac{3}{25}$ _____

23. $\frac{7}{20}$ _____

24. $\frac{19}{50}$ _____

Write each percent as a fraction in lowest terms.

25. 64% _____

26. 36% _____

27. 50% _____

28. 2% _____

29. 80% _____

30. 44% _____

31. 60% _____

32. 12% _____

33. 85% _____

34. 72% _____

35. 96% _____

36. 8% _____

37. 39% _____

38. 55% _____

39. 35% _____

40. $37\frac{1}{2}$% _____

41. 20% _____

42. 25% _____

43. 30% _____

44. $12\frac{1}{2}$% _____

45. 86% _____

46. 98% _____

47. 10% _____

48. $87\frac{1}{2}$% _____

Large and Small Percents

Express each percent as a decimal.

1. 350% _____ **2.** 2.25% _____ **3.** 400% _____

4. $4\frac{1}{4}$% _____ **5.** 160% _____ **6.** 7.4% _____

7. 950% _____ **8.** 645% _____ **9.** $3\frac{1}{2}$% _____

10. $\frac{1}{2}$% _____ **11.** 0.7% _____ **12.** 575% _____

13. 1.2% _____ **14.** 315% _____ **15.** 720% _____

Express each decimal as a percent.

16. 8.0 _____ **17.** 2.68 _____ **18.** 0.005 _____

19. 7.4 _____ **20.** 0.0075 _____ **21.** 9.3 _____

22. 3 _____ **23.** 0.003 _____ **24.** 0.123 _____

25. 5.82 _____ **26.** 0.065 _____ **27.** 4 _____

28. 3.62 _____ **29.** 0.053 _____ **30.** 6.29 _____

Express each fraction as a percent.

31. $\frac{180}{100}$ _____ **32.** $\frac{624}{100}$ _____ **33.** $\frac{429}{100}$ _____

34. $\frac{7}{4}$ _____ **35.** $\frac{5}{2}$ _____ **36.** $\frac{13}{10}$ _____

37. $\frac{17}{10}$ _____ **38.** $\frac{11}{4}$ _____ **39.** $\frac{6}{5}$ _____

40. $\frac{3.25}{100}$ _____ **41.** $\frac{0.4}{100}$ _____ **42.** $\frac{0.25}{100}$ _____

Using Percents: Finding a Percent of a Number

Find the percent of each number. Use a decimal for the percent.

1. 67% of 60 _____

2. 5% of 40 _____

3. 106% of 700 _____

_____

_____

_____

4. 15% of 264 _____

5. 12% of 50 _____

6. 65% of 84 _____

_____

_____

_____

Find the percent of each number. Use a fraction for the percent.

7. 25% of 152 _____

8. 75% of 428 _____

9. $33\frac{1}{3}$% of 69 _____

_____

_____

_____

10. 50% of 486 _____

11. 20% of 465 _____

12. 30% of 70 _____

_____

_____

_____

Solve. Use either method.

13. 1% of 389 _____

14. 10% of 389 _____

15. 100% of 389 _____

16. 25% of 66.4 _____

17. 65% of 72 _____

18. 9.2% of 185 _____

19. $12\frac{1}{2}$% of 480 _____

20. 150% of 76 _____

21. 112% of 450 _____

22. 48% of 48 _____

23. 160% of 25 _____

24. $37\frac{1}{2}$% of 64 _____

25. 110% of 90 _____

26. 0.3% of 150 _____

27. 80% of 250 _____

28. 150% of 105 _____

29. 1.5% of 105 _____

30. 15% of 105 _____

Using Percents: Finding What Percent
One Number Is of Another

Find the percents.

1. What percent of 75 is 45?

_____

2. What percent of 108 is 81?

_____

3. 5 is what percent of 40?

_____

4. 8 is what percent of 50?

_____

5. What percent of 140 is 21?

_____

6. What percent of 200 is 88?

_____

7. What percent is 9 out of 300?

_____

8. What percent is 31 out of 200?

_____

9. What percent of 292 is 73?

_____

10. What percent of 40 is 3?

_____

11. 40 is what percent of 25?

_____

12. 36 is what percent of 20?

_____

13. What percent of 600 is 54?

_____

14. What percent of 500 is 310?

_____

15. What percent is 11 out of 88?

_____

16. What percent is 82 out of 123?

_____

Name _____

Using Critical Thinking

Express each ratio as a lowest-terms fraction, as a percent, and as a decimal.

1. 24 out of 100

_____

2. 48:200

_____

3. 75:100

_____

4. 30 parts to 36 parts

_____

Express each percent as a decimal and as a lowest-terms fraction.

5. 85%

_____

6. 46%

_____

7. 14%

_____

8. $66\frac{2}{3}\%$

_____

9. 1%

_____

10. 0.4%

_____

11. Find 125% of 6.

_____

12. What is 12% of 1?

_____

13. What percent of 3 is 6?

_____

14. 14 is what percent of 84?

_____

15. $\frac{1}{5}\%$ of 20 is what number?

_____

16. Find 0% of 1.

_____

17. If 6 is 10% of 60, then

12 is _____ of 60

18 is _____ of 60

24 is _____ of 60

18. If x is $y\%$ of z, then

$3x$ is _____ of z

$4x$ is _____ of z

$5x$ is _____ of z

Name _____

Using the Strategies

Solve. Use any problem solving strategy.

1. Refer to the table at the right. What is the mean of the percent of electricity generated by nuclear power plants in the five countries? Express your answer as a percent and as a lowest-terms fraction.

Percent of electricity generated by nuclear power plants in 1988	
United States	20%
Switzerland	37%
Sweden	47%
Belgium	66%
France	70%

_____

2. What percent of the electricity generated in Belgium was from sources other than nuclear power plants?

_____

3. The Metropolis Fire Department conducted a drive to raise $15,000 to purchase a "Jaws of Life." They reached 115% of their goal. How much money did they raise?

_____

4. The typical American family uses 12% of its water for laundry, 15% for bathroom sinks, 40% for toilets, 20% for baths, 10% for kitchen uses, and the remainder for outdoor uses. What percent is used for outdoor uses? Express your answer as a percent and as a decimal.

_____

5. What percent of water is used inside the house? Express your answer as a percent, a decimal, and a lowest-terms fraction.

Using Percents: Finding a Number When a Percent of It Is Known

Solve.

1. $25\% \times n = 19$

2. $50\% \times n = 47$

3. $5\% \times n = 6$

_____

_____

_____

4. $10\% \times n = 11$

5. $150\% \times n = 36$

6. $400\% \times n = 84$

_____

_____

_____

7. $66\% \times n = 99$

8. $8\% \times n = 10$

9. $19\% \times n = 57$

_____

_____

_____

10. $12\% \times n = 21$

11. $22\% \times n = 33$

12. $15\% \times n = 24$

_____

_____

_____

Find the number.

13. 25% of what number is 34?

14. 18% of what number is 45?

_____

_____

15. 45% of what number is 9?

16. 50% of what number is 9.2?

_____

_____

17. 6% of what number is 0.9?

18. 120% of what number is 558?

_____

_____

19. 75% of what number is 138?

20. 150% of what number is 249?

_____

_____

21. 8% of what number is 1.2?

22. 160% of what number is 152?

_____

_____

Name _____

Commission

Use a calculator to find the commission. Round to the nearest cent.

1. house sale: $149,900
commission rate: 5%

_____

2. furniture sale: $2,762.99
commission rate: 3%

_____

3. car sale: $18,750
commission rate: 6%

_____

4. house sale: $325,000
commission rate: 4.5%

_____

5. stock sale: $330,000
commission rate: 9%

_____

6. boat sale: $28,456.79
commission rate: 12%

_____

7. jewelry sale: $4,015
commission rate: 20%

_____

8. car sale: $9,852.99
commission rate: 7%

_____

9. house sale: $167,900
commission rate: 5.5%

_____

10. furniture sale: $486.95
commission rate: 2%

_____

11. ticket sale: $258.93
commission rate: 3.5%

_____

12. jewelry sale: $1,963.48
commission rate: $2\frac{1}{2}\%$

_____

13. house sale: $88,450
commission rate: 5.6%

_____

14. furniture sale: $1,214.56
commission rate: 4.4%

_____

Name _____

Percent of Increase and Decrease

Find the percent of increase or decrease. Round to the nearest tenth when needed.

1. Lee bought a bicycle for $40. After making some repairs, he sold the bicycle for $70.

_____

3. Jessie scored 6 points in the first half of the basketball game. She scored 15 points in the second half of the game.

_____

2. The average temperature for August was 90° F. The average temperature for September was 75° F.

_____

Sandy made this chart of her expenses for April and May. Complete the chart.

	Expense	April	May	Increase or Decrease	Amount	Percent
4.	Travel	$ 40	$ 50			
5.	Food	225	189			
6.	Entertainment	45	99			
7.	Rent and Utilities	360	378			
8.	Clothing	155	62			
9.	Other	135	108			
10.	Total	960	886			

Solve.

11. D and L Painters' profits were $25,000 last year. This year, they are up $5,000. Welty Plumbing's profits went down $16,000 last year to $20,000 this year. What were the amount and percent of increase for each business?

_____

_____

12. A coat was priced at $150 in a store. The coat cost the owner of the store $90. What is the owner's percent of markup?

_____

Name _____

Using the Strategies

To solve these problems you can Draw a Picture,
Solve a Simpler Problem, Make a Table, Look for a
Pattern, or use another strategy. Tell which strategy
you used.

1. A football team has 11 players. In how many
different ways can they line up for the bus?

_____

Strategy: _____

_____

_____

2. The Antico family sat at the home team's 20-yard
line. The Greenbergs sat at the visitors' 30-yard
line. If both families sat on the same side of the
field, how many yards apart were they?

_____

Strategy:

_____

_____

3. An adult's ticket for the game costs $4.50, a child's
ticket costs $2.50, and a senior citizen's ticket
costs $3.00. If Mrs. Rodriguez spent exactly $20.00,
what combinations of tickets could she buy?

Strategy:

_____

_____

Discounts and Sale Prices

Find the discount and sale price.

1. Regular Price: $130
   Discount Percent: 10%

   Discount: _____

   Sale Price: _____

2. Regular Price: $36
   Discount Percent: $33\frac{1}{3}$%

   Discount: _____

   Sale Price: _____

3. Regular Price: $60
   Discount Percent: 40%

   Discount: _____

   Sale Price: _____

4. Regular Price: $20
   Discount Percent: 15%

   Discount: _____

   Sale Price: _____

5. Regular Price: $160
   Discount Percent: 25%

   Discount: _____

   Sale Price: _____

6. Regular Price: $125
   Discount Percent: 20%

   Discount: _____

   Sale Price: _____

7. Regular Price: $64
   Discount Percent: $12\frac{1}{2}$%

   Discount: _____

   Sale Price: _____

8. Regular Price: $300
   Discount Percent: 15%

   Discount: _____

   Sale Price: _____

9. Regular Price: $410
   Discount Percent: 8.5%

   Discount: _____

   Sale Price: _____

10. Regular Price: $12.50
    Discount Percent: 10%

    Discount: _____

    Sale Price: _____

Permutations

Solve.

1. The numbers on the cards can be used to form 4-digit numbers. How many 4-digit numbers are possible?

_____

6. There are 4 women on a relay team. How many ways can the coach set the order in which they will run?

_____

2. 9 tennis players are competing for 2 trophies. How many different ways can the trophies be awarded?

_____

7. 12 persons tried out for 2 openings on the tennis team. How many permutations of the 2 chosen players are there?

_____

3. 4 friends are in line for movie tickets. How many different ways could they be in line?

_____

8. A plant, a book, a record, and a tape were door prizes at a party. There were 10 people at the party. How many different ways can the prizes be given?

_____

4. 5 people enter a room, one at a time. In how many different orders can they enter the room?

_____

9. Jack has 6 books he wants to read. In how many different orders can he read the books?

_____

5. There are 8 entries in a horse show class, competing for 3 ribbons. In how many ways can the ribbons be awarded?

_____

10. 14 people tried out for the lead and understudy in a play. How many different ways can the parts be assigned?

_____

Problems with More than One Answer

Solve. Use any problem solving strategy.

1. A rectangular deck has an area of 36 ft². Fill in the table to show all possible whole number dimensions and perimeters of the deck.

Dimension (in feet)	Perimeter (in feet)

2. The perimeter of a triangle is 27 cm. The longest side is 2.5 cm shorter than twice the length of the shortest side. The remaining side is 1.5 cm longer than the shortest side. What are the dimensions of the triangle?

_____

3. The Ace Realty Company sold 5 houses in one week. The sale prices were $114,000, $123,999, $256,500, $76,150, and $192,899. What was the average price of the houses sold by Ace that week?

_____

4. At a commission rate of 6%, how much commission did Ace Realty earn on the sales of the 5 houses?

_____

5. Ms. Avia was Ace's best salesperson that week. She sold the three most expensive homes. Her commission was $\frac{1}{6}$ the commission earned on the sale of the three homes. How much did Ms. Avia earn that week?

_____

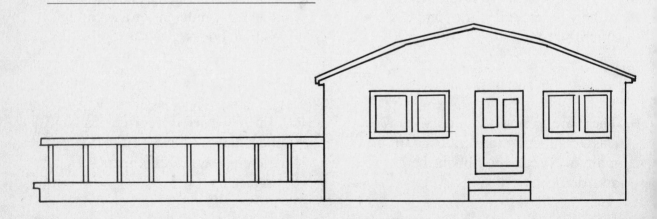

Name _____

Choosing a Calculation Method

Choose mental math, pencil and paper, or a calculator
to solve each problem.

1. Lee bought computer paper for $15.00,
disks for $25.00 and folders for $10.00.
How much did he spend?

_____

2. Erin bought her supplies at a discount
store. She spent $13.79 for paper,
$21.45 for disks and $7.53 for folders.
How much did she spend?

_____

3. Beno is paid $3.50 an hour at his part
time job. One week he worked 10
hours. How much did he make?

_____

4. Stella is paid $4.52 per hour at her part
time job. One week she worked 12.5
hours. How much did she earn?

_____

5. Sue is making a pen for her dog. It will
be a square pen with a side of 3.7 m.
What is the perimeter of the pen?

_____

6. Jared is making a rectangular garden.
His garden will be 5 feet, 3 inches long
and 4 feet, 9 inches wide. What is the
perimeter of his garden?

_____

7. Jacque lost his calculator. What method
might he use to find the total cost of a
new calculator at $13.99 and a tax of
$1.12?

_____

8. If he decides on a calculator that costs
$17.59, a calculator book that is $7.88,
and the tax is $1.78, what method
might he use to find the total cost?

_____

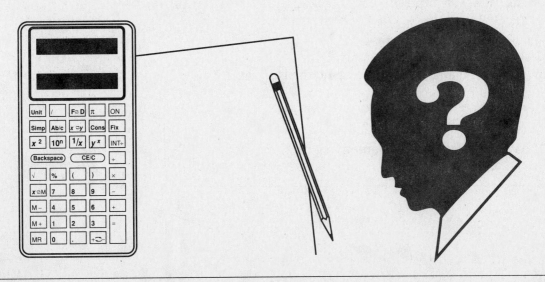

Basic Geometric Concepts

Use the figure at the right to name the following:

1. An obtuse angle _____

2. Two acute angles _____

3. Two right angles _____

4. Two pairs of supplementary angles _____

_____

5. A pair of complementary angles

_____

6. The measure of $\angle TRU$ _____

7. The measure of $\angle TRV$ _____

Give the measure of a complement to the given angle.

8. $m\angle X = 20°$ _____   **9.** $m\angle A = 48°$ _____   **10.** $m\angle T = 72°$ _____

Give the measure of a supplement to the given angle.

11. $m\angle Z = 10°$ _____   **12.** $m\angle C = 37°$ _____

13. $m\angle N = 115°$ _____   **14.** $m\angle E = 144°$ _____

Lines a and b are parallel.

15. Name the angles with the same measure as $\angle 7$.

_____

16. What angles are supplementary to $\angle 2$?

_____

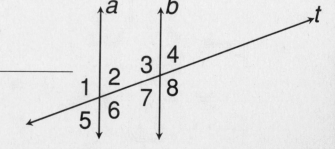

Name _____

Pentomino Polygons

Find the sum of the turn angles for each polygon.

1.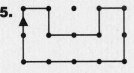

2.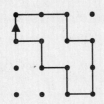

3.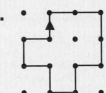

4.

_____   _____   _____   _____

5.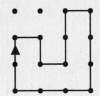

6.

7.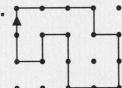

8.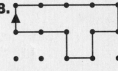

_____   _____   _____   _____

Find the sum of the vertex angles for each of the
polygons in Exercises 1–8.

9. Ex. 1   **10.** Ex. 2   **11.** Ex. 3   **12.** Ex. 4

_____   _____   _____   _____

13. Ex. 5   **14.** Ex. 6   **15.** Ex. 7   **16.** Ex. 8

_____   _____   _____   _____

Find the sum of the turn angles when you go around
each polygon in the direction of the arrow.

17.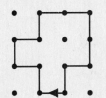

18.

19.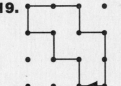

20.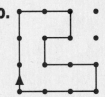

_____   _____   _____   _____

Name _____

Polygons

Name each polygon. Find the sum of the measures of
the vertex angles.

1.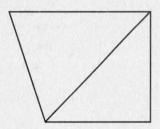

_____

2.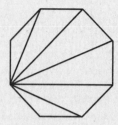

_____

3.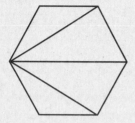

_____

4.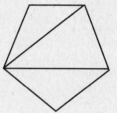

_____

Find m ∠ x in each polygon.

5.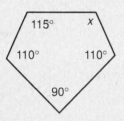

_____

6.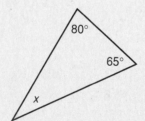

_____

7.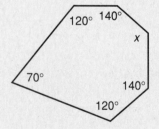

_____

8.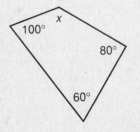

_____

9.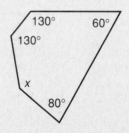

_____

Name _____

Circles

Use the circle to answer Exercises 1–7.

1. Name three radii of the circle.

_____

2. Name a diameter of the circle. _____

3. Name two central angles of the circle.

_____

4. Name two arcs with *M* as one end.

_____

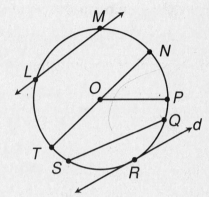

5. Name two chords of the circle.

_____

6. Name a secant line. _____

7. Name a tangent line. _____

The two circles in the figure are concentric circles
with center at *P*.

8. Name three radii of the small circle.

_____

9. Name three radii of the large circle.

_____

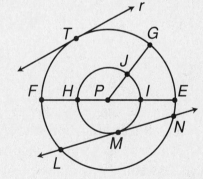

10. Name a diameter of the small circle.

_____

11. Name a diameter of the large circle.

_____

12. Name a tangent line of the large

circle. _____

13. Name a tangent of the small circle.

_____

14. If the length of $\overline{PH}$ is 1 cm, what is

the length of $\overline{HI}$? _____

Using the Strategies

Solve. Use any problem solving strategy.

1. A ball is dropped from a height of 16 meters. On each bounce the ball reaches $\frac{1}{2}$ the height of its previous bounce. How high will it go on its fourth bounce?

_____

2. A square and a triangle have the same perimeter. The dimensions of the triangle are 3 cm, 4 cm, and 5 cm. How long is each side of the square?

_____

3. To the nearest million, find the mean of the populations of Florida (11.2 million), Iowa (2.8 million), California (26.3 million), and Texas (16.3 million).

_____

4. Pedro is on the track team. He trains $1\frac{1}{4}$ hours every weekday and $1\frac{3}{4}$ hours on Saturday and Sunday. How many hours does he train each week?

_____

5. Lucy bought a dress, regularly priced at $69.99, on sale for 30% off. How much did she pay?

_____

6. In how many ways can the 6 teams in a hockey league finish 1st through 5th?

_____

7. A patio is in the shape of a hexagon. Each side is 8 feet long. There is a flower planter at each vertex and every 4 feet in between. How many planters are there?

_____

Name _____

Parallel and Perpendicular Lines

In the figure at the right, $\overleftrightarrow{MB}$ and $\overleftrightarrow{NT}$ are parallel
lines. $\overleftrightarrow{AS}$ is perpendicular to $\overleftrightarrow{NT}$ and $\overleftrightarrow{MB}$.

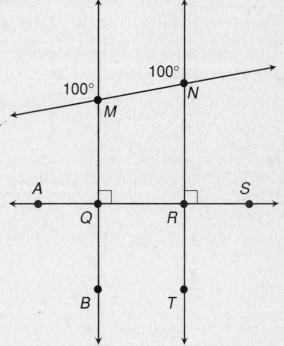

1. Name two transversals of $\overleftrightarrow{MB}$ and $\overleftrightarrow{NT}$.

_____

2. Name two transversals of $\overleftrightarrow{MN}$ and $\overleftrightarrow{AS}$.

_____

3. Name 8 right angles.

_____

_____

4. What is the measure of $\angle MNR$?

_____

5. How many other angles have the

same measure as $\angle MNR$? _____

6. What is the measure of $\angle NMQ$?

_____

Use a compass and a straightedge to do the following
constructions.

7. Draw line *l* and construct a line *m*
parallel to line *l*.

8. Draw a line *s*. Mark a point *P*.
Construct a line *t* through *P*
perpendicular to line *s*.

Constructing Angle and Segment Bisectors

Use a compass and straightedge to do each
construction.

1. Construct the bisector of ∠LMN.

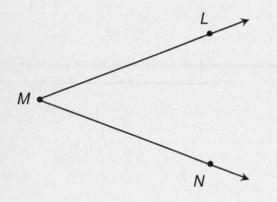

2. Construct the bisector of ∠CJG.

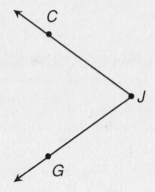

3. Construct the bisector of each of the three angles of the triangle.

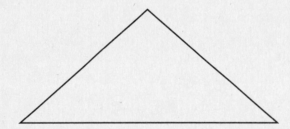

4. Construct the perpendicular bisector of each side of the triangle.

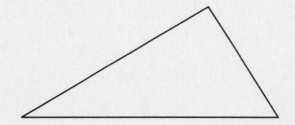

Data from a Menu

To solve problems involving restaurant dining, you may need to refer to data from a menu.

1. Lee and Lyle were mighty hungry when they sat down to order at Mama's BBQ. Lee ordered the beef plate à la carte, two orders of chili, cole slaw, and soup. Lyle ordered exactly the same thing but substituted potato salad for the cole slaw. Including tax of 6%, how

much did their meal cost? _____

2. Feeling very satisfied after their meal, Lee and Lyle left a tip of 20% of the total check. How much was their tip?

_____

3. Mike T. Gray comes in regularly at Mama's BBQ at 5:00 p.m. for his Sunday night meal. He orders the one whole chicken and soup. Taking the senior citizen's discount, what is the

cost of his meal before tax? _____

4. Including 6% tax and a 15% tip on the meal and tax, how much does Mike T.

Gray spend? _____

5. Bill E. Boy washes dishes at Mama's BBQ. After work he gets a free meal. He orders the three-meat combo à la carte and chili. Including tax of 6%,

what would his meal cost? _____

Plates: all plates are served with green salad and one muffin à la carte: meat portion only.

	Plates	A La Carte
Chicken	$3.85	$3.25
Link	3.95	3.35
Beef	4.35	3.75

Combinations:	Plates	A La Carte
Two-meat combo	$5.85	$5.25
Three-meat combo	7.85	7.25

Weekend Specials   3 p.m. to 10 p.m.

Half-a-chicken: includes 2 corn muffins and potato salad	$ 4.20
One whole chicken: includes 3 corn muffins and potato salad	$ 7.35
Rack-o-ribs: includes 4 corn muffins and potato salad	$12.40
Chili	$ 1.05
Cole slaw	$ 1.25
Potato salad	$ 1.25
Steaming Hot Soup	$ 1.05

SENIOR CITIZEN'S DISCOUNT

10% discount on all purchases.

Exploring Algebra: More on Graphing Functions

Complete the tables of (x,y) values for the given
values of x and graph the functions.

1. $y = x^2 - 5$ for $x = {}^-5, {}^-4, {}^-3, {}^-2, {}^-1, 0,$
    $1, 2, 3, 4, 5, 6$

2. $y = x^3 + 2$ for $x = {}^-3, {}^-2, {}^-1, 0, 1, 2, 3$

x	y
$^-5$	
$^-4$	
$^-3$	
$^-2$	
$^-1$	
0	
1	
2	
3	
4	
5	

x	y
$^-3$	
$^-2$	
$^-1$	
0	
1	
2	
3	

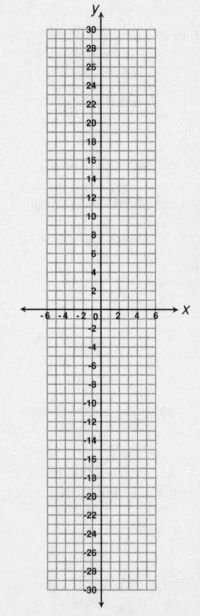

Square Roots and Irrational Numbers

Each decimal has a pattern in its digits. Give the next
3 digits in the pattern. Tell if the number is **rational** or
irrational.

1. 0.424242 . . . _____

2. 0.3456 . . . _____

3. 6.010010001 . . . _____

4. 0.81818 . . . _____

5. 5.555 . . . _____

6. 0.3444 . . . _____

7. 0.213141 . . . _____

8. 0.121231234 . . . _____

9. 0.2334445 . . . _____

10. 0.071071 . . . _____

11. 0.243243 . . . _____

12. 0.00450045 . . . _____

Find the repeating decimal for each rational number.

13. $\frac{9}{11}$ _____

14. $\frac{1}{6}$ _____

15. $\frac{1}{3}$ _____

16. $\frac{2}{9}$ _____

17. $\frac{1}{12}$ _____

18. $\frac{5}{99}$ _____

19. $\frac{11}{37}$ _____

20. $\frac{6}{11}$ _____

21. $\frac{4}{33}$ _____

22. $\frac{5}{12}$ _____

23. $\frac{2}{3}$ _____

24. $\frac{5}{22}$ _____

25. $\frac{7}{111}$ _____

26. $\frac{4}{9}$ _____

27. $\frac{9}{66}$ _____

Express each square root as a decimal rounded to the
nearest thousandth. Tell if it is **rational** or **irrational.**

28. $\sqrt{71}$ _____

29. $\sqrt{122}$ _____

30. $\sqrt{32}$ _____

31. $\sqrt{18}$ _____

32. $\sqrt{441}$ _____

33. $\sqrt{48}$ _____

34. $\sqrt{67}$ _____

35. $\sqrt{361}$ _____

36. $\sqrt{1,700}$ _____

37. $\sqrt{53}$ _____

Name _____

Exploring Algebra: Solving Inequalities by the Addition Property

Solve and graph these inequalities.

1. $x + 3 < 40$

_____

2. $y - 12 > 13$

_____

3. $^-5 \leq a + 3$

_____

4. $n - 23 > ^-12$

_____

5. $m + ^-4 \leq ^-6$

_____

6. $y - 12 \geq ^-0.4$

_____

7. $t + 4 > \sqrt{16}$

_____

8. $v - \sqrt{9} \geq \sqrt{25}$

_____

9. $^-4 \leq m - 2.3$

_____

10. $0.94 + b < 2.76$

_____

11. $^-4\frac{7}{8} + n \geq ^-3\frac{1}{2}$

_____

12. $\sqrt{36} < x + 16$

_____

13. $6 \leq 10 + y$

_____

14. $8.4 > 5.3 + c$

_____

15. $x - 6 < -4$

_____

Name _____

Using Critical Thinking

Here are two ways of using a scale to weigh a pound
of sand.

A Use a 1-pound weight on one side of
the scale and balance the other side
with sand.

B Use an ounce weight on one side of the
scale and balance the other side with
sand. Since there are 16 ounces in a
pound, repeat the weighing 16 times.

1. Which weighing is more likely to be awkward? ___

2. If the process of weighing is awkward, is it likely to

be less accurate? _____

Greater accuracy is more likely if an appropriate tool
is used to do the job. Ring the measuring instrument
that is likely to be most accurate.

3. Timing an olympic swim race

  A wristwatch with an accurate second
hand

  B stopwatch measuring in tenths of
seconds

4. Measuring a room for a new rug

  A yardstick

  B 25-yard measuring tape

5. Weighing a newborn baby

  A scale measuring in pounds

  B scale measuring pounds and ounces

6. Fitting parts together on a model
airplane

  A ruler measuring in sixteenths of an
inch

  B ruler measuring in fourths of an inch

Name _____

Using the Pythagorean Relationship

Find the length of hypotenuse c or missing leg for each right triangle. Round to the nearest thousandth if necessary. Use a table of square roots or a calculator.

1.

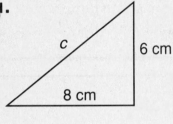

$c =$ _____

2.

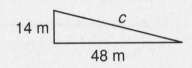

$c =$ _____

3.

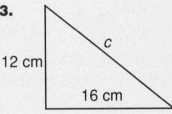

$c =$ _____

4.

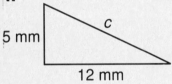

$c =$ _____

5.

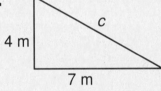

$c =$ _____

6.

$c =$ _____

7. $a = 24$ m
   $b = 32$ m

$c =$ _____

8. $a = 6$ mm
   $c = 7.810$ mm

$b =$ _____

9. $a = 3$ km
   $b = 2$ km

$c =$ _____

10. $a = 7$ dm
   $b = 3$ dm

$c =$ _____

11. $b = 4$ m
   $c = 5.657$ m

$a =$ _____

12. $a = 40$ cm
   $b = 50$ cm

$c =$ _____

13. $a = 30$ km
   $b = 30$ km

$c =$ _____

14. $a = 20$ cm
   $b = 60$ cm

$c =$ _____

15. $a = 15$ m
   $c = 25$ m

$b =$ _____

16. $a = 4$ m
   $b = 9$ m

$c =$ _____

17. $c = 28.284$ m
   $b = 20$ m

$a =$ _____

18. $a = 2$ cm
   $b = 9$ cm

$c =$ _____

Name _____

Using the Strategies

Solve. Use any problem solving strategy.

1988 Statistics

	U.S.A.	Japan	U.S.S.R.	W. Germany
Population (millions)	247.498	123.231	287.015	60.162
Life expectancy (years)	75	78	69	75
Average workweek (hours)	41	46.8	39	40.5
Unemployment rate	5.5%	2.5%	n.a.	8%
Household income (1 year)	$30,759	$38,200	$8,700	$20,875

1. Find the mean and the mode of the life expectancy in the 4 countries.

_____

_____

2. What percent of the U.S.A. household income was the income in the U.S.S.R.?

_____

3. If the average American worked 48 weeks per year, how many hours did he or she work?

_____

4. Can you find the average weekly income for workers from each country?

_____

_____

_____

_____

If the average worker in each country worked approximately 50 years, with 2 weeks vacation each year, about how many hours would he or she work in a lifetime?

5. U.S.A. _____ h

6. Japan _____ h

7. U.S.S.R. _____ h

8. W. Germany _____ h

45°-45° Right Triangles

Find the length of the hypotenuse of each 45°-45°
right triangle. Express your answer both in radical
form and as a decimal approximation to the nearest
thousandth.

Use $\sqrt{2} \approx 1.414$.

1.

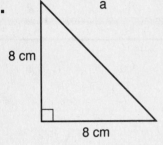

8 cm

8 cm

a

2.

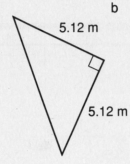

b

5.12 m

5.12 m

3.

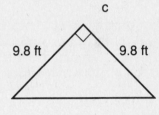

c

9.8 ft   9.8 ft

_____   _____   _____

Find the length of the hypotenuse (h) or leg (a or b)
for each 45°-45° right triangle. Round to the nearest
thousandth.

4. $a = 24$ m
    $b = 24$ m

    $h \approx$ _____

5. $a = 20$ cm
    $b = 20$ cm

    $h \approx$ _____

6. $a = 11$ cm
    $h \approx 11\sqrt{2}$ cm

    $b =$ _____

7. $b = 14$ m
    $h \approx 19.796$ m

    $a =$ _____

8. $a = 32$ cm
    $b = 32$ cm

    $h \approx$ _____

9. $h \approx 15\sqrt{2}$ in
    $a = 15$ in

    $b =$ _____

10. $a = 25$ dm
    $b = 25$ dm

    $h \approx$ _____

11. $b = 9$ m
    $a = 9$ m

    $h \approx$ _____

12. $a = 13$ cm
    $b = 13$ cm

    $h \approx$ _____

13. $h \approx 20\sqrt{2}$ m
    $a = 20$ m

    $b =$ _____

14. $a = 5$ m
    $h \approx 7.070$ m

    $b =$ _____

15. $b = 18$ cm
    $a = 18$ cm

    $h \approx$ _____

30°-60° Right Triangles

Find *x* and *y* for each triangle. Express answers in
radical form.

1.

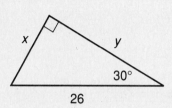

2.

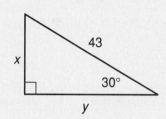

3.

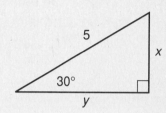

x = _____   *x* = _____   *x* = _____

y = _____   *y* = _____   *y* = _____

Use the 30°-60° right triangle to find *a*, *b*, or *c*.

4. If *c* = 15, find *a* and *b*.

_____

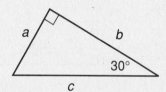

5. If *c* = 25, find *a* and *b*.

_____

6. If *c* = 100, find *a* and *b*.

_____

7. If *a* = 13.2, find *b* and *c*.

_____

8. If $b = 99\sqrt{3}$, find *a* and *c*.

_____

9. If *c* = 2.3, find *a* and *b*.

_____

10. If $c = \sqrt{9}$, find *a* and *b*.

_____

11. If *a* = 2, find *b* and *c*.

_____

12. If $b = 21\sqrt{3}$, find *a* and *c*.

_____

13. If $b = 2\sqrt{3}$, find *a* and *c*.

_____

14. If *c* = 0.04, find *a* and *b*.

_____

Name _____

Problem Solving: Using a Calculator

Solve. Use any problem solving strategy. Use your
calculator. Express answers to the nearest tenth.

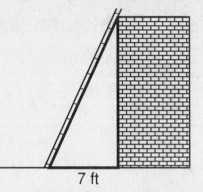

1. If the ladder in the drawing is 28 feet
long, how high is the wall?

_____

7 ft

2. Suppose the ladder is 40 ft long and it
is 36.7 ft from the ground at the bottom
of the wall to the top of the ladder.
What is the distance from the bottom
of the ladder to the wall?

_____

3. Mohsen leaned a 36-foot ladder against
the wall. He placed the bottom of the
ladder 9 feet out from the bottom of
the wall. He climbed halfway up the
ladder to reach a kite. How far from the
ground was Mohsen?

_____

4. Helene bought a box of paper clips. She
paid $2.10, including 5% sales tax. If
each clip cost $0.02 before tax, how
many clips were in the box?

_____

5. A basketball court is 78 feet long and
has an area of 2,808 square feet. What
is the diagonal distance across the
court?

_____

Name _____

Translations

Draw the translation image of each polygon.

1.

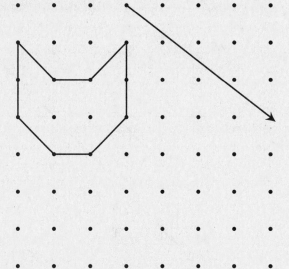

2.

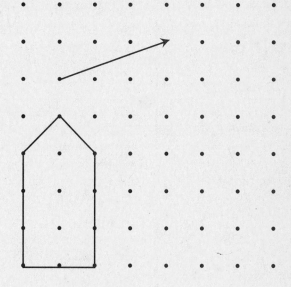

3. Complete the translation image at the right. Identify the coordinates of the translation image at each point.

4. $A(^-8,^-1) \rightarrow$ _____

5. $B(^-6,0) \rightarrow$ _____

6. $C(^-4,3) \rightarrow$ _____

7. $D(^-1,^-2) \rightarrow$ _____

8. $E(^-4,^-6) \rightarrow$ _____

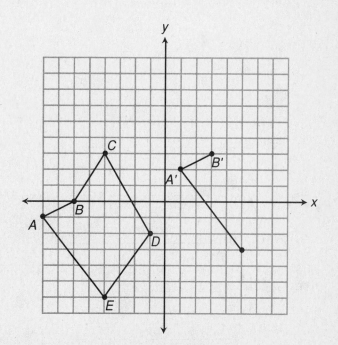

Name _____

Reflections

Draw the reflection image of each polygon.

1.

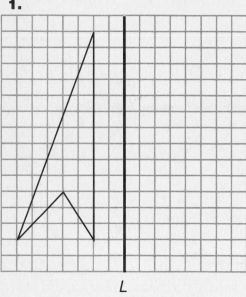

L

2.

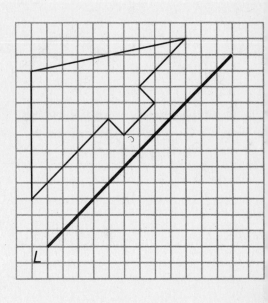

L

3. Draw the reflection image at the right. Identify the coordinates of the reflection image of each point.

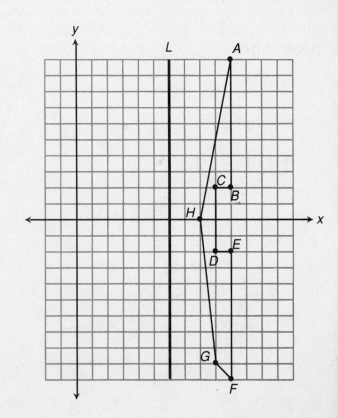

4. A(10,10) _____

5. B(10,2) _____

6. C(9,2) _____

7. D(9,⁻2) _____

8. E(10,⁻2) _____

9. F(10,⁻10) _____

10. G(9,⁻9) _____

11. H(8,0) _____

Name _____

Rotations

Draw the $\frac{1}{4}$ turn image of each figure with turn center at (0,0).

1.

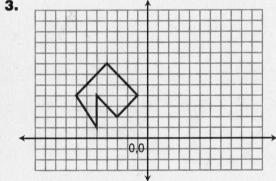

2.

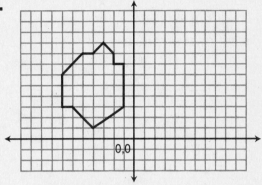

3.

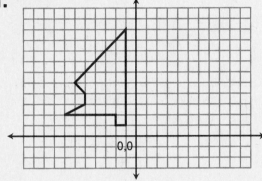

4.

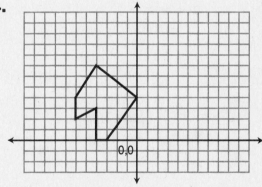

For each point, find the coordinates of the $\frac{1}{4}$ turn image with turn center at (0,0). Use the L-shaped line to visualize the rotation image.

5.

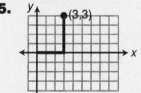

(3,3)

6.

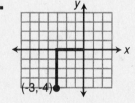

(-3,-4)

7.

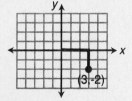

(3,-2)

8.

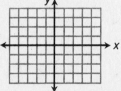

(2,-4)

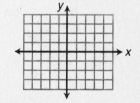
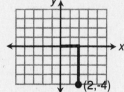

Name _____

Symmetry

Identify the type or types of symmetry for each figure or pattern. If a figure or pattern has reflectional symmetry, identify at least one line of symmetry. If it has rotational symmetry, identify whether it has $\frac{1}{4}$, $\frac{1}{2}$, or $\frac{3}{4}$ rotational symmetry.

1.

_____

2.

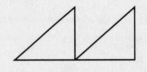

_____

3.

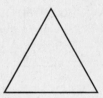

_____

4.

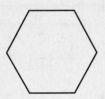

_____

5.

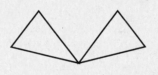

_____

6.

_____

7.

_____

8.

_____

9.

_____

Name _____

Congruent Figures

Match congruent figures, if possible.

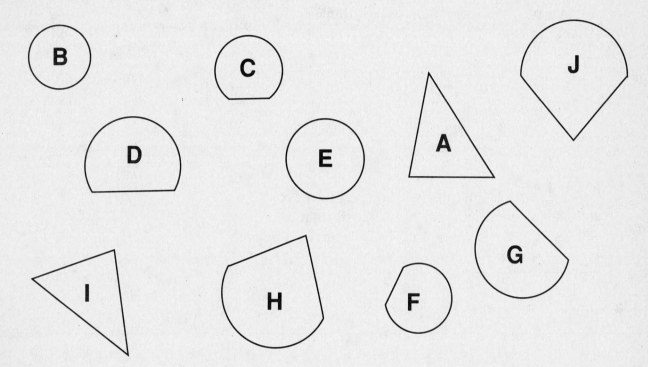

1. Figure A   **2.** Figure B   **3.** Figure C   **4.** Figure D   **5.** Figure E

    Figure _____   Figure _____   Figure _____   Figure _____   Figure _____

6. Figure F   **7.** Figure G   **8.** Figure H   **9.** Figure I   **10.** Figure J

    Figure _____   Figure _____   Figure _____   Figure _____   Figure _____

11. Draw the translation image of the figure at the right for the translation that moves (x, y) to $(x + 3, y - 3)$. Give the coordinates for both figures.

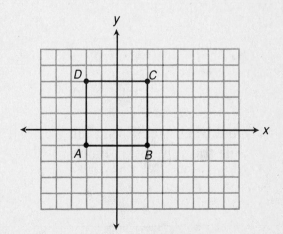

12. A _____ A' _____

13. B _____ B' _____

14. C _____ C' _____

15. D _____ D' _____

Name _____

Using Critical Thinking

1. Imagine that you rotate this number around the decimal point $\frac{1}{2}$ turn. What do you think will be the result?

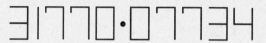

_____

2. Look again at the number with respect to the x and y axes. What two successive transformations will result in the same message as in Exercise 1?

_____

3. Draw the two transformation images.

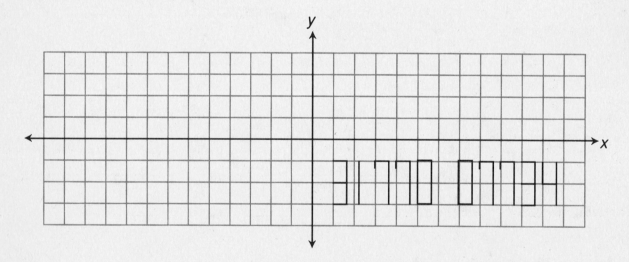

4. What single transformation would result in the same transformation image in the same location as in Exercises 2 and 3?

_____

Exploring Algebra: Graphing Two Linear Equations

Complete each table.

1.

x	y
3	7
4	9
5	11
6	___

2.

x	y
1	4
2	3
3	2
4	___

3.

x	y
2	3
3	5
4	7
5	___

Match the following with the correct patterns from problems 1, 2, and 3.

4. $y = 2x - 1$ _____

5. $y = 2x + 1$ _____

6. $y = 5 - x$ _____

Graph the pairs of equations. If the lines intersect, give the coordinates of the point of intersection.

7. $y = 3$
$x = 4$

_____

8. $y = x$
$y = x - 3$

_____

9. $y = 2x + 2$
$y = {}^-x + 5$

_____

10. $y = x + 3$
$y = x - 1$

_____

11. $y = x + 1$
$y = 3$

_____

12. $y = 2x$
$y = 3x$

_____

Decide whether each ordered pair is on the graph of the equation or inequality.

13. $y = 7x + 23$
$(4, 51)$

_____

14. $y > 3.5x - 12$
$(13, 45)$

_____

15. $y \geq 5x + 2$
$(6, 20)$

_____

Name _____

Using the Strategies

Patty runs a small ceramics business. Four employees form an assembly line to make teapots. First John makes the body of the teapot by throwing it on a pottery wheel. Luis then forms a handle and attaches it to the body. Next Allie shapes and attaches a spout. Finally Monte measures the opening of the teapot and makes a lid on another pottery wheel. It takes 10 minutes for each person to complete his or her step.

Finish drawing the teapots at each stage of completion in the chart below. Use it to help fill in the table and answer the questions.

	John	Luis	Allie	Monte
10 minutes	(body)			
10 minutes	(body)	(handle)		
10 minutes	(body)		(spout)	
10 minutes	(body)			(lid)

Number of completed teapots	Length of time to complete
1	
2	
3	
4	
5	
6	

1. After 1 hour how many pots has John thrown? _____

2. After 1 hour how many handles has Luis attached? _____

3. After 1 hour how many teapots are complete except for a lid? _____

4. If the assembly line continues at the same pace, when 6 teapots are complete, how many pots has John thrown? _____

5. How long does it take for them to complete 12 teapots? _____

6. The assembly line takes a break after an hour and a half. How many teapots are in an incomplete stage? _____

Name _____

Constructing Congruent Segments and Angles

Construct a congruent copy of each figure.

1. $\angle A \cong \angle V$

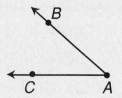

2. $\angle J \cong \angle E$

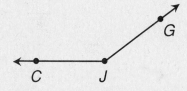

3. $\angle D \cong \angle Q$

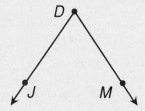

4. $\overline{VM} \cong \overline{V'M'}$

5. $\overline{KJ} \cong \overline{SH}$

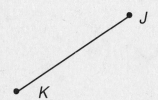

Congruent Triangles

List the pairs of congruent sides and angles for each
pair of congruent triangles.

1.

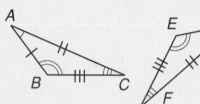

_____

_____

_____

2.

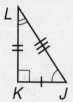

_____

_____

_____

Write a statement of congruence for each pair of
congruent triangles.

3.

_____

4.

_____

5.

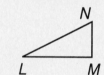

_____

6.

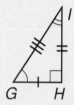

_____

7. Find x and y.

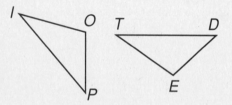

$x =$ _____ $y =$ _____

8. Write a statement of congruence.

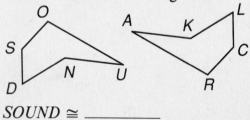

$SOUND \cong$ _____

SAS and ASA Congruence

Use a compass and a straightedge to do each construction.

1. Use SAS congruence to construct a triangle congruent to △*XYZ*.

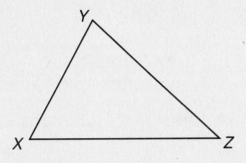

2. Use ASA congruence to construct a triangle congruent to △*LMN*.

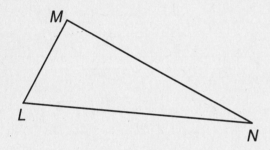

3. Construct a triangle that has sides congruent to the three segments.

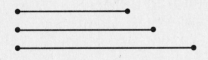

4. Construct a triangle that has two sides and the included angle congruent to the sides and angle below.

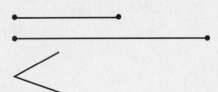

Name _____

Developing a Plan

Solve. Use any problem solving strategy.

1. Jo and Flo collect posters of movie stars. Moe
   agreed to sell his collection to the girls. He agreed
   to charge Jo $3 for each poster. Flo agreed to pay
   $0.03 for the first poster, $0.06 for the second,
   $0.12 for the third, and so on, doubling the price
   for each poster. Complete the tables to see which
   girl has the best arrangement.

Poster number	Jo pays	Accumulated total
1	$3	$3
2	$3	

Flo pays	Accumulated total
$0.03	$0.03

2. Which girl pays less? _____

3. Continue the table to find out which girl would
   pay less if they bought 5 more posters each.

4. Which girl pays less? _____

Poster number	Jo pays	Accumulated total

Flo pays	Accumulated total

Using Critical Thinking

1. What are the next 4 square numbers following

100? _____

2. Of the next 4 square numbers following 100, which

▶ has the largest number of 2-factors? _____

▶ have the same number of 2-factors? _____

▶ have half squares that are integers? _____

3. Why do you think the half squares of 11 and 13 are not integers?

_____

4. Do the 4 additional cases help to prove the argument that a square number always has an even number of 2-factors?

_____

_____

_____

5. How could you either prove or disprove this statement?

Since all square numbers always have an even number of 2-factors, any number with an even number of 2-factors must be a square number.

_____

_____

_____

Name _____

Verifying Conjectures by Reasoning

Evaluate the expression to complete the table. Then
answer the questions.

1.

x	$x + x - 1$
1	
2	
3	
4	
5	

4.

t	$t^2 + t^2$
1	
2	
3	
4	
5	

2. In the table 1 above did you get any
even numbers? _____

5. In the table above did you get any odd
numbers? _____

3. Do you think that for any x you would
get an even number? Why?

_____

_____

_____

_____

6. Do you think that for any t you would
get an odd number? Why?

_____

_____

_____

_____

7. Two people meet and shake hands. There is one
handshake. If three people meet and all shake
hands there would be three handshakes. Use the
diagrams below to help complete the table for 4
and 5 people.

2 people

1 handshake

3 people

3 handshakes

Number of people	Number of handshakes
2	1
3	3
4	
5	

Reasoning in Algebra

Write an algebraic explanation for each number trick.

1. Choose any number between 0 and 10.

Add 10.   _____

Multiply by 2.   _____

Divide by 4.   _____

Subtract 5.   _____

Multiply by 2.   _____

Is the answer the original number?   _____

2. Choose an even number between
   0 and 10.

Add 14.   _____

Multiply by 2.   _____

Subtract 8.   _____

Divide by 4.   _____

Subtract $\frac{1}{2}$ the original number.   _____

What is the answer?   _____

3. Marlo has 5 envelopes and 17 sheets of paper. How can she put an odd number of sheets in each envelope?

_____

_____

4. How could Marlo put 53 sheets of paper in 5 envelopes with an odd number in each envelope?

_____

_____

Name _____

Reasoning in Geometry

Find the perimeters. Assume all "cut aways" are rectangles.

1.

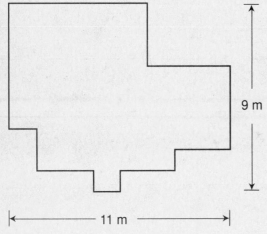

9 m

|← 11 m →|

2.

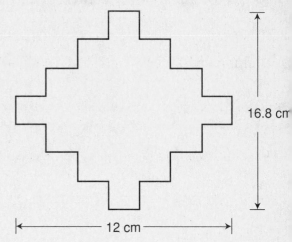

16.8 cm

|← 12 cm →|

Find the area of each figure below.

Figure 1

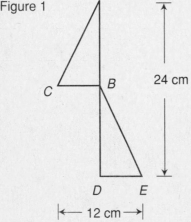

24 cm

|← 12 cm →|

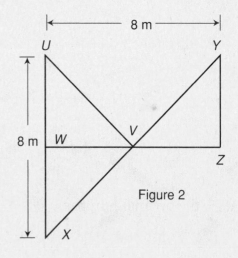

|← 8 m →|

8 m

Figure 2

6. area △ *UWV* = _____

3. area △ *BDE* = _____

7. area △ *XWV* = _____

4. area △ *ABC* = _____

8. area △ *YZV* = _____

5. area Figure 1 = _____

9. area Figure 2 = _____

Name _____

Reasoning from Graphs

Use the axes below to plot points on a graph to fit
the story.

There are 230 eighth graders in Sil's school. He
decided to draw a graph predicting the number of
eighth graders watching television each hour of one
weekday. He figured most students get up around
6:30 a.m. and some will watch an early-morning show
before going to school. During school hours only
those who are home sick will be watching TV. After-
school programs start around 3:30 and last until
about 5:30. Prime time for watching TV usually
begins around 7:30 and reaches a peak between 8:00
and 9:00. As bedtime approaches most will turn off
the TV but a few students will be late-night TV
watchers.

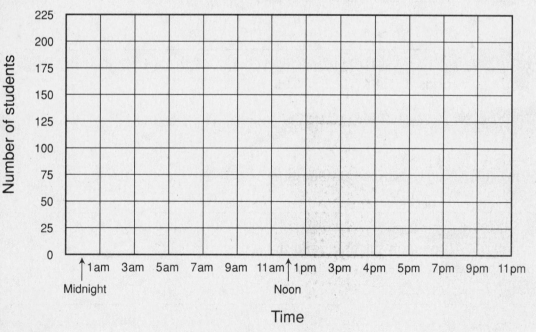

Eighth Graders Watching T.V.

Make up a story for a Sunday TV viewing schedule.
Use a different color to plot the points on the graph
above.

Name _____

More Reasoning with Graphs

The graph shows some changes in the stock market in
recent years.

Recent Stock Market Values

1. During which 2-month period did the value of the

   stock market decrease the most? _____

2. Following the decrease described in Question 1,
   how long did it take for the stock market to regain

   all its lost value? _____

3. During how many periods in 1988 was the slope

   of the graph positive? _____

4. What was happening to the value of the stock
   market during the periods described in Question 3?

   _____

5. During what periods shown on the graph did the
   slope remain positive the longest?

   _____

6. During the period June–July 1988, how would you
   describe what was happening to the value of the
   stock market?

   _____

Name _____

Estimating the Answer

Estimate the answer. Then solve the problem. Use
any problem solving strategy.

1. The Royal Corporation has 884
employees. The president wants to
arrange vacation time so that the
same number of employees vacation
each of the 52 weeks of the year. How
many employees should take vacation
each week?

   _____

2. 286 of the 884 employees ride the
train to work. How many employees
do not ride the train?

   _____

3. Van pools are used by 88 employees.
If a van can carry 8 people, how
many vans go to Royal Corporation?

   _____

4. During one week the number of
employees off sick was: Monday 28,
Tuesday 34, Wednesday 25, Thursday
38, Friday 40. What was the total
number of sick days taken?

   _____

5. It cost the company $28 per employee
for the annual awards party. If 714
employees attended, what was the cost
of the party?

   _____

6. The lunchroom at Royal Corporation
has 95 tables. If there are 6 chairs at
each table, how many employees may
eat at the same time?

   _____

7. The Royal Corporation office supplies
budget is $1,000 per week. The office
manager has spent $116, $384, and
$221 so far this week. How much is
left for supplies this week?

   _____

8. The company is giving $176,800 in
bonuses to its employees. How much
will each of the 884 employees get if
the bonus money is evenly divided?

   _____

9. The Royal Corporation bought a
$9,320 machine that was on sale for
$8,550. How much did they save by
buying the machine on sale?

   _____

10. The Royal Corporation has a training
program for its sales force that costs
$1,700 per person. How much will it
cost for 22 employees to be in the
program?

   _____